The Antichrist Arises Out Of Europe And Is About To Appear On The World Scene!

Roger Henri Trepanier

© 2022

This book is dedicated to KJ Ozborne, who is a believer,
a video producer, and former US Coast Guard Medic,
who seeks to make The Lord Jesus Christ known in the
world, and as such deserves our support!
Of such believers, God says:

"A faithful man will abound with blessings…"

Proverbs 28:20

Titles available from Roger Henri Trepanier in The Truth Seeker's Library™ series:

God Did Not Create Human Beings To Die… But To Live On… Eternally!
Finding Comfort And Encouragement In The Promises Of God In The Last Days
How We Know For Sure That We Are Living In The Last Days!
Have You Ever Wondered What Happens After Death?
An Introduction To The New World That Is Coming On The Earth
Deeper Truths Of The Christian Life
Evangelism As God Intended
Keeping On Serving God In The Last Days
The Mysterious World Of Angels And Demons
No One Loves As He Loves!
Thanks Be To God For His Indescribable Gift!
The Church Is Very Much Alive, Well, And Growing!
Tracing The Steps Of The Son Of God From Eternity To Eternity!
War, And Going To War, Is Simply Not Of God!
God Never Meant Prayer To Be A Mystery!
Health Is One Of God's Great Blessings!
Removing The Mystery Surrounding Baptism!
This World's Return To Paganism Is Almost Complete!
Removing The Mystery Surrounding Heaven!
God's Covenants Were Meant For Mankind's Blessing!
The Four Ages Of Time
The Awesomeness Of God!
A Call To A Biblical Christianity!
Believers! Look Up! Our Homegoing Is Any Day!
Why God Created The Male And The Female!
This Earth Was Never Meant To Be The Believer's Home!
It Is A Terrifying Thing To Fall Into The Hands Of The Living God!
The Rapture Of The Church Is God's Last End Time Event!

Titles available from Roger Henri Trepanier in The Practical Helps Library™ series:

Learning to Overcome The Perplexities Of This Present Life
So, I Hear You Want To Work With Seniors?
I Will Not Have This Man To Rule Over Me!
Spiritual Truth To Warm The Heart!

Fasten Your Seatbelts: Turbulence Ahead!
Living A Normal Christian Life In An Increasingly Abnormal World!
If You Have Jesus; You Do Not Need Drugs!
To Do God's Will Is To Have A Foretaste Of Heaven!
This World Is Ready For The Rule Of The Antichrist!
President Trump And The Q Movement Versus Satan And The DEEP STATE
More Of God's Great Promises For Comfort And Encouragement!
Alert! The C-Virus Pandemic Was Satan's Practice Run For A New World Order
The Days Are Evil! The Time Is Short! Be Saved From This Perverse Generation!
Your Worldview Determines Your Wellbeing And Eternal Destiny!
What We Are Watching Is The Spirit Of The Antichrist At Work!
A Sure Cure For Loneliness!
Will God Allow President Trump To Regain The White House?

Titles available from Roger Henri Trepanier in The Christian Fiction Library™ series:

The Beginning Of A New Dawn
It Is Never Too Late For Love!
The True To Life Musings Of Fred And Ernie
Between A Rock And A Hard Place!
Love Knows No Boundaries!
A Woman Worth Pursuing!
Love Is More Than Just A Four Letter Word!
The Twists And Turns Of The Life Of Faith!

Titles available from Roger Henri Trepanier in The Word Of God Library™ series:

God's First Letter To The Thessalonians
God's Second Letter To The Thessalonians
God's Letter To Believers Through Jude
God's Three Short Letters To Believers Through John
God's Letter To Scattered Believers Through James
God's Letter To Titus
God's Prophetic Word To Mankind Through Daniel
God's Letter To Philemon And God's Letter To The Colossians
God's Consummation Of All In The Book Of Revelation
God's Letter To The Philippians

God's First Letter Through Peter
God's Second Letter Through Peter
Jonah, God's Reluctant Prophet!
God's Letter To The Galatians
God's Providence In The Book Of Esther
God's Love For Gentiles In The Book Of Ruth
God's Letter To The Ephesians
God's First Letter To Timothy
God's Second Letter To Timothy
Jesus' Sermon On The Mount: Matthews 5 to 7
Jesus" Parting Words Of Love To His Own: John 13 To 16
God's Letter To The Romans
God's Letter To The Hebrews

INTRODUCTION

This book is being written with two main purposes in mind. The first is that a lot of people, mostly believers, appear to be confused as to WHO the antichrist will be that God says in His word is coming on the world scene after this present third age has ended. And so, our first purpose will be to present information regarding the coming antichrist which is in line with what God has disclosed in His word, the Bible, regarding this coming evil world leader!

And our second purpose relates to the fact that there is also a lot of people, and again mostly believers, who do not appear to know that the antichrist MUST arise out of present-day Europe, which will therefore again necessitate presenting the truth that God has disclosed in His word on this subject, therefore showing that the antichrist indeed arises out of a revived Roman Empire, which is present day Europe! We will also endeavor to put forth truth regarding this evil character, who by all appearances of what is going in the world, will soon be making his appearance on the world scene as the antichrist!

What we will also do in this book is look at the present alignment of the nations of the world, which will be shown to be in line with Revelation 6 and the military conflicts that occurs on earth as soon as the present third age ends, which immediately ushers in the rule of the antichrist on the world scene!

What should also be noted is that at the back of the book there is an Addenda with three sections. In Addendum A, there is a brief outline of the four ages of time, for any reading the book who might not be familiar with this information. In Addendum B, there is a brief outline of the two comings from Heaven to earth in time of God's Son, The Lord Jesus Christ, for any who may not be familiar with this information either. And then in Addendum C, we have a presentation of the gospel, which is the good news that God has given in His word regarding His Son, The Lord Jesus Christ, for any readers who might not have as yet this vital personal relationship with God, through faith in His Son.

What should also be mentioned before closing this Introduction, because we are all somewhat curious by nature, is that after completing 21 years of formal education and then spending almost

28 years working in Project Engineering and Management in the Corporate offices of two large utilities, God called His servant as a non-denominational evangelist in early 1999, and then sent him out over two thousand miles, away from family and friends, to the place of service God assigned, which is where His servant has been, and is still serving Him, as evangelist, author, and counselor. The author is a widower with three adopted children, all now married with a family of their own.

Please note the two websites listed below, which have been established for the purpose of interacting with readers and for gospel ministry:

http://www.pilgrimpathwaypublications.com

http://servantofmosthigh.com

And now my prayer is that God will richly bless you as you read this book, and greatly minister to every need in your life, as only God can! To Him be all praise, honor, and glory, with thanksgiving, both now and forevermore! Amen.

CONTENTS

Page

Introduction

The Antichrist Arises Out of Europe And Is About To Appear On The World Scene!

Chapter One — What God has in view when He speaks of the "antichrist" and the "spirit of the antichrist" in His word!...... 15

Chapter Two — The devil has been attempting since ancient times to bring an evil ruler on the world scene to rule over all mankind, and will one day succeed with his antichrist! 21

Chapter Three — Seeing from God's word at Daniel 2 and 9 that the antichrist does indeed arise out of a revived Roman Empire, which is present day Europe! 41

Chapter Four — Seeing from God's word that the present third age of time was never seen during the second age of time, and so, when God resumes the second age in order to complete the last seven years of it, there will be no knowledge of this present third age!!.... 75

Chapter Five — The present-day alignment of the nations of the world is exactly in line with the military conflicts we see occurring at Revelation 6, which is when the antichrist makes his entry on the world scene! 81

Chapter Six — Ten things the devil needs to have in place in order to bring his evil agenda to pass on earth! 93

Addendum A	The four ages of time	99
Addendum B	The two comings from Heaven to earth of God's Son, The Lord Jesus Christ	105
Addendum C	For those who may not as yet know God	109
Next Book		115

"Children, it is the last hour; and just as you heard that ANTICHRIST is coming, even now MANY ANTICHRISTS HAVE APPEARED; from this we know that it is THE LAST HOUR."

1 John 2:18

"By this you know the Spirit of God: every spirit that confesses that Jesus Christ has come in the flesh is from God, and every spirit that does not confess Jesus is not from God; this is THE SPIRIT OF THE ANTICHRIST, of which you have heard that it is coming, and now it is already in the world."

1 John 4:2,3

CHAPTER ONE

/ What God has in view when He speaks of the "antichrist" and the "spirit of the antichrist" in His word!

The term 'antichrist'

It is most likely that everyone has heard the term 'antichrist' at one time or another. However, unless one reads the Bible, where God makes this known, one might just know that this is a term that God uses to refer to someone who opposes 'Christ.' If that is your present understanding of "antichrist," then at least you know the basic meaning of the term.

However, in order to better understand the times we live in, and especially come to realize that there are unseen forces of evil in operation behind the scenes, which not only explains all that is presently going on in the world at this time, but also explains what has been going on since the dawn of mankind on earth, let us go on to look in more detail at a verse that God gives to help explain this subject, which is one we used as a quote to precede this chapter, which is 1 John 2:18, where we read, "Children, IT IS THE LAST HOUR; and just as you heard that ANTICHRIST IS COMING, even now MANY ANTICHRISTS HAVE APPEARED; from this WE KNOW THAT IT IS THE LAST HOUR."

There are three very important truths that God tells us relating to the antichrist in this verse. The first is that there is a PERSON coming on the world scene in time, who will be called, "ANTICHRIST." Secondly, God tells us that even now, during the present third age of time, there are "MANY ANTICHRISTS," meaning that there are many human beings now on earth who exhibit the same evil characteristics that this person, who will be the antichrist, will himself exhibit when he does appear on the world scene!

Then the third very important truth that God makes known to us here is that it is now "THE LAST HOUR," speaking of the fact that we have reached the end of the present third age. In other words, the present age is just about to end, with very little time left. And the reason that God gives for our knowing that it is "the last hour," is that "many antichrists have appeared." In other words, just from the fact that so many people the world over oppose God's eternal Son, Jesus Christ, is proof that we are very close to the end of the present third age of time!

The term 'the spirit of the antichrist'

And that leads us to that other term that God uses in His word, which is "the spirit of the antichrist," which is found at 1 John 4:2,3, which was also quoted to precede this chapter, and where we read, "[2] By this you know the Spirit of God: every spirit that confesses that Jesus Christ has come in the flesh is from God; [3] every spirit that does not confess Jesus is not from God; THIS IS THE SPIRIT OF THE ANTICHRIST, of which you have heard THAT IT IS COMING, and now IS ALREADY IN THE WORLD."

God here again discloses two very important truths to us. The first is that God gives a test for believers to use for determining if one is speaking by The Holy Spirit, and therefore a believer, or whether one is simply speaking from one's human spirit as an unbeliever. And the reason why God gives this test is that only believers, as those who have The Holy Spirit indwelling in one's human spirit from the moment of one's salvation onward, will be able to confess, "that Jesus Christ has come in the flesh," simply because this is a truth that only The Holy Spirit can make known to a person. And so, unbelievers, in not having The Holy Spirit, because never having believed in God's Son for salvation, will never confess or acknowledge as an inward reality "that Jesus Christ has come in the flesh."

Then the second very important truth here is that God defines for us what "the spirit of the antichrist" is, which is "every spirit that does not confess Jesus." Based on what we have said above, this then means that every person on earth, who is not a believer, in terms of never having come to personally know God in salvation, to receive from Him the forgiveness of sins and eternal life with Him, has "the spirit of the antichrist." That "spirit of the antichrist" is already in the world simply because the majority of people alive in this world at any one time during the present third age are unbelievers.

And please understand here that all human beings start life in this world as unbelievers, from the age of accountability onward! All human beings are born innocent as babies, not knowing good or evil. However, there comes a day, known only to God, which is the age of accountability, where He tests every person, after He knows that a person has come to know good and evil. And when one chooses the evil, then one has personally sinned against God for the first time and is now personally accountable to God!

What this also means is that from then on one has not only activated one's sinful nature inherited from Adam, and passed on through the conception of the female since then, but one has also sided with the devil, who led Adam and Eve into sin in the first place (noting Genesis 3:1-6). And in siding with the devil against God in sinning that first sin renders one not only an unbeliever in need of redemption from then on, but also renders one in God's sight as an "antichrist" and as one with "the spirit of antichrist."

"For many deceivers have gone out into the world, those who do not acknowledge Jesus Christ as coming in the flesh. This is the deceiver and THE ANTICHRIST."

2 John 1:7

CHAPTER TWO

/ The devil has been attempting since ancient times to bring an evil ruler on the world scene to rule over all mankind, and will one day succeed with his antichrist!

What we will look at in this chapter is the fact that the devil has been at work since the dawn of history in trying to establish A ONE WORLD GOVERNMENT on earth, which WOULD BE UNDER HIS DIRECT CONTROL. We are to also be aware of the fact that God has revealed in his word, the Bible, that just as He has established a Kingdom, which has His Son as King, and which is presently being populated with believers; so too with Satan, the devil, will also be seen as seeking during the ages of time to establish his own kingdom on earth, with the antichrist as king over it, with unbelievers as its subjects!

So let us go on now to look at two passages of God's word – one from the Old Testament period, and one from the New Testament, to see that the devil indeed has the goal of bringing a leader on the world scene, who would be under his authority and ruling over all mankind on earth, and that he will eventually be successful when he does bring the antichrist on the world scene!

Satan's attempt through Nimrod at the beginning of time to establish a one world leader on earth!

And so, let us begin with an event from Old Testament Biblical history, which occurred after the worldwide flood, where we see a rebellion take place against God on earth under the leadership of a man named "NIMROD," who sought to build for himself a kingdom on earth in opposition to God, noting what we read to begin with at Genesis 10:8,10-12, "[8] Now Cush became the father of NIMROD, HE BECAME A MIGHTY ONE ON THE EARTH… [10] THE BEGINNING OF HIS KINGDOM WAS BABEL and Erech and Accad and Calneh, IN THE LAND OF SHINAR. [11] From that land he went forth into Assyria, and built Nineveh and Rehoboth-Ir and Calah, [12] and Resen between Nineveh and Calah; that is the great city."

Then let us go on and read from Genesis 11:1-9, where we see the unbelievers of earth, as led by Nimrod, be in a rebellion against God, there seeking to establish a worldwide empire, as we there read, with capitalization and notes in brackets added as a help, "[1] Now THE WHOLE EARTH used THE SAME LANGUAGE and the same words. [2] It came about as THEY journeyed east, that THEY found a plain IN THE LAND OF SHINAR and settled there. [3] THEY said to one another, "Come, let us make bricks and burn them thoroughly." And they used brick for stone, and they used tar for mortar. [4] They said, "COME, LET US BUILD FOR OURSELVES A CITY, AND A TOWER WHOSE TOP WILL REACH INTO HEAVEN, AND LET US MAKE FOR OURSELVES A NAME, otherwise we will be scattered abroad over the face of the whole earth." [5] The Lord came down to see the city and the tower which the sons of men (in unbelief) had built. [6] The Lord said, "Behold, THEY ARE ONE PEOPLE, AND THEY ALL HAVE THE SAME LANGUAGE. And this is what they began to do, and now nothing which they purpose to do will be impossible for them. [7] Come, let Us (in reference to God The Father, His Son, and The Holy Spirit) go down and there confuse their language, so that they will not understand one another's speech." [8] So the Lord scattered them abroad from there over the face of the whole earth; and they stopped building THE CITY. [9] Therefore its name was called BABEL, because there the Lord confused the language of the whole earth; and from there the Lord scattered them abroad over the face of the whole earth."

So here we see that this unbeliever, Nimrod sought to build a kingdom on earth, starting at a city, which became known as "Babel," and which later in history became Babylon. There, with the consent of the other unbelievers of earth, they sought to build a tower reaching into heaven, which was a declaration of not only wanting to be equal with God, but to actually replace God over the peoples of the earth! Their wanting to make a name for themselves in building this city and this tower meant a display of unbridled pride! And we now need to spend a few moments discovering that this sinful pride was actually derived from Satan, the devil, who was actually behind all their worldly efforts!

Satan's fall due to the sin of pride!

For what we now need to note is that when the devil was created by God, he was a sinless angelic being, who had access to the very Presence of God, along with all the other angelic beings. However, there came a day when PRIDE did take over in him and he sinned against God, then becoming Satan, the devil, who then led a third of the other angelic beings in rebellion against God, before then leading our first parents, Adam and Eve, into sin here on earth!

So let us note to begin with what God tells us about the fall of this angelic being into sin, who after he sinned became, Satan, the devil, noting now what God tells us of him at Isaiah 14:12-14, especially noting his five "I will" here, "[12] How you have fallen from heaven, O star of the morning, son of the dawn! You have been cut down to the earth, you who have weakened the nations! [13] But you said in your heart, 'I WILL ascend to heaven; I WILL raise my throne above the stars of God, And I WILL sit on the mount of assembly in the recesses of the north. [14] I WILL ascend above the heights of the clouds; I WILL make myself like the Most High."

Then let us note what God goes on to tell us at Ezekiel 28:12-17 in part, regarding that angelic being who became Satan, the devil, there reading, "[12] You had the seal of perfection, full of wisdom and perfect in beauty. [13] You were in Eden, the garden of God; every precious stone was your covering… On the day that you were CREATED they were prepared. [14] You were the anointed cherub (an order of angelic beings with a higher rank than ordinary angels) who covers, and I placed you there. You were on the holy mountain of God; you walked in the midst of the stones of fire. [15] YOU WERE BLAMELESS IN YOUR WAYS FROM THE DAY YOU WERE CREATED UNTIL UNRIGHTEOUESNESS (the sin of pride) WAS FOUND IN YOU. [16] By the abundance of your trade you were internally filled with violence, and YOU SINNED, therefore I have cast you as profane from the mountain of God. And I have destroyed you, O covering cherub, from the midst of the stones of fire. [17] YOUR HEART WAS LIFTED UP BECAUSE OF YOUR BEAUTY, YOU CORRUPTED YOUR WISDOM BY REASON OF YOUR SPLENDOR…"

From the verses in Isaiah and also from Ezekiel here, we see that from the time of his own fall into sin, which was due to pride, the devil has had the ambition to not only be like God, in terms of also having a kingdom on earth, but of actually having his throne higher than God's throne, so as to rule not only over Him, but also over all of God's original creation!

Satan seen as one day finally bringing his antichrist on the world scene in time!

Since the devil later saw that God was ruling over His kingdom through His Son, Who was the visible expression of Himself, Who was always invisible; as assisted by The Holy Spirit; then the devil sought to establish his own kingdom on earth, as he eventually will do, as we will now clearly see from the next passage that we need to look at here, which is Revelation 13 in God's word, the Bible. And please note that this will be taking place during the last seven years left of the second age of time. In other words, as soon as this present third age ends, God resumes the second age to complete the last seven years of it, and this is when the antichrist will now be ruling on earth over a one world government!

What we will do here then is to look at Revelation 13:1-10 to begin with, which is the first three and half years of that seven year period, with notes added in brackets as a help, including capitalizing certain words for emphasis, "[1] And the DRAGON (who is devil here, noting Revelation 12:9) stood on the sand of the seashore. Then I saw a BEAST (the antichrist) coming up out of the sea (speaking of one of the nations of the earth), having ten horns and seven heads, and on his horns were ten diadems, and on his heads were blasphemous names. [2] And the beast which I saw was like a leopard, and his feet were like those of a bear, and his mouth like the mouth of a lion. AND THE DRAGON (the devil) GAVE HIM (the antichrist) HIS POWER AND HIS THRONE AND

GREAT AUTHORITY. [3] I saw one of his heads AS IF IT HAD BEEN SLAIN, AND HIS FATAL WOUND WAS HEALED. AND THE WHOLE EARTH (of unbelievers) WAS AMAZED AND FOLLOWED AFTER THE BEAST (the antichrist); [4] they (the unbelievers of earth) worshiped the dragon (the devil) because he gave his authority to the beast (the antichrist); and they worshiped the beast, saying, "Who is like the beast, and who is able to wage war with him?" [5] There was given to him (the antichrist) a mouth speaking arrogant words and blasphemies, and authority to act for FORTY-TWO MONTHS (which is three and half years, keeping in mind that in God's word, a month has 30 days) was given to him. [6] And HE (the antichrist) OPENED HIS MOUTH IN BLASPHEMIES AGAINST GOD, to blaspheme His name and His tabernacle, that is, those who dwell in heaven. [7] It was also given to him TO MAKE WAR WITH THE SAINTS (the believers of earth, who will have been saved by God at the start of that seven year period) and to overcome them, and AUTHORITY OVER EVERY TRIBE AND PEOPLE AND TONGUE AND NATION WAS GIVEN TO HIM (therefore seeing here that the antichrist rules as political ruler over all the peoples of the earth, bar none). [8] All (unbelievers) who dwell on the earth will worship him, everyone whose name has not been written from the foundation of the world in the book of life of the Lamb who has been slain. [9] If anyone has an ear, let him hear. [10] If anyone is destined for captivity, to captivity he goes; if anyone kills with the sword, with the sword he must be killed. Here is the perseverance and the faith of the saints."

There are a number of truths that we need to grasp in order to understand what God is saying to us here, specifically relating to the coming antichrist. The first is that Revelation 13 deals with the time period that the antichrist will actually be on earth, which as we have said is during the last seven years remaining of the second age of time, which begins immediately after the close of the present third age, as when God resumes the second age in order to now complete it!

Secondly, we need to see that the "dragon" mentioned at Revelation 13:1 here is actually Satan, the devil, as is clear from God identifying him as such at Revelation 12:9, there saying, "And the great dragon was thrown down, the serpent of old who is called the devil and Satan, who deceives the whole world; he was thrown down to the earth, and his angels (fallen angels, who are evil spirits known as demons) were thrown down with him."

Then thirdly, relating specifically to our present purpose, we are to see from verse 2b and the last part of verse 7, that the dragon, who is Satan, the devil, gives the beast, who is the antichrist, "his power and his throne and great authority." It is at this time that the antichrist will rule over a one world government that will be over all the nations on earth, as is clear from what God says here, "authority over every tribe and people and tongue and nation was given to him," with that rule being by all the power that the devil himself has, being under his direct authority!

And fourthly, we are to see from verses 3,4, and 8 that all unbelievers of earth, bar none, will not only follow after the beast, who is the antichrist, but will also worship him and the dragon, who is the devil. And from verse 5, we are to see that the antichrist will be ruling over all the unbelievers of earth directly for "forty-two months," which is the first three and half years of the last seven years remaining of the second age of time, keeping in mind that God is here using a Biblical month, which has 30 days, so that 42 months divided by 12 months to the year is three and half years.

We are also to note a fifth truth from the first part of verse 7, which is that the antichrist will be allowed, which is by God here, "to make war with the saints and to overcome them." The "saints" here in view are the believers of the earth who will be saved at the start of the last seven years, as part of a large ingathering by God during this time, as is clear from what God tells us at Revelation 7:9,10,13,14.

And let us keep in mind here that Revelation 6:1 to Revelation 19:21 is a detailed account given by God of what takes place on earth and in Heaven during the last seven years left of the second age of time, which is often referred to as 'the tribulation period,' simply because it is a time of tribulation for the believers, who will be on earth during this seven year period, for as we see from the first part of Revelation 13, the believers of earth will be under constant persecution by the antichrist during this three and half year period, and also in the next three and a half year period when the false prophet comes on the scene, as we will see in a moment!

And before leaving for the moment this brief introduction to this passage, let us also note that the last seven years of the second age begins with the antichrist going out and making war, as is clear from what God says at the end of verse 4, and also based on what we read of him at Revelation 6:2, which is relating to the antichrist at the start of his rule on earth at the beginning of that seven year period, "I looked, and behold, a white horse, and he who sat on it had a bow; and a crown was given to him, and he went out conquering and to conquer." The "crown" here indicates the fact of the antichrist's rule over the nations of the earth!

Let us now remember this important information as we briefly turn to look at a third evil character that God introduces us to here at Revelation 13, which we need to be familiar with if we are to fully understand the true identity of the antichrist and to grasp Satan's objectives, since the antichrist is at all times under his direct authority for all he thinks, does, and says during the seven year time period that he will be ruling over the nations of the earth.

And now we will look at the rest of Revelation 13, namely verses 11 to 18, which is the last three and a half years of the seven years left of the second age of time, where we see that the antichrist will now be assisted on earth by the religious leader, who will be over a one world religion on earth, this being the second beast in view here, also known as 'the false prophet' (noting Revelation 19:20; 20:10). This false prophet will be under the antichrist, who will still be the political leader during the last three and half years, with both of these evil characters being under the direct authority of the devil.

And so, let us note what we now read at Revelation 13:11-18, "[11] Then I saw ANOTHER BEAST (the false prophet) coming up out of the earth; and he had two horns like a lamb and he spoke as a dragon. [12] HE EXERCISES ALL THE AUTHORITY OF THE FIRST BEAST (the antichrist) IN HIS PRESENCE. And he makes the earth and those who dwell in it to worship the first beast (the antichrist), whose fatal wound was healed. [13] He (the false prophet) performs great signs, so that he even makes fire come down out of heaven to the earth in the presence of men. [14] And he deceives those who dwell on the earth (the unbelievers) because of the signs which it was given him to perform in the presence of the beast (the antichrist), telling those who dwell on the earth (the unbelievers) to make an image to the beast (the antichrist) who had the wound of the sword and has come to life. [15] And it was given to him to give breath to the image of the beast, so that the image of the beast would even speak and cause as many as do not worship the image of the beast to be killed. [16] And he causes all, the small and the great, and the rich and the poor, and the free men and the slaves, to be given a mark on their right hand or on their forehead, [17] and he provides that no one will be able to buy or to sell, except the one who has the mark, either the name of the beast (the antichrist) or the number of his name. [18] Here is wisdom. Let him who has understanding calculate the number of the beast (the antichrist), for the number is that of a man; and his number is six hundred and sixty-six."

And again here, we need to grasp a number of truths in order to understand what God is telling us. The first is that this second beast, mentioned at verse 11, is referred to by God as being "the false prophet" at Revelation 16:13; 19:20; and 20:10. Then at verse 12, we are clearly told that this second beast, who is the false prophet, "exercises all the authority of the first beast in his presence," and what we are to see by this is that while the antichrist is still on earth as POLITICAL LEADER, the false prophet is on earth under the authority of the antichrist as RELIGIOUS LEADER over a one world false religion! And of course, both are still under the direct authority and power of the devil.

Then we are to also carefully note what we were told at verse 3 above regarding the first beast, who is the antichrist, "I saw one of his heads as if it had been slain, and his fatal wound was healed. And the whole earth was amazed..." And then, we are told at verse 12 and 14 in this regard, "And he (the second beast, who is the false prophet) makes the earth and those who dwell in it to worship the first beast (who is the antichrist), whose fatal wound was healed... telling those who dwell on the earth to make an image to the beast who had the wound of the sword and has come to life." The obvious question here is: What is the meaning of this? And the answer is that in knowing what this means we learn of the true identity of the antichrist and the objectives that the devil has, in the devil raising both the antichrist and the false prophet at this time in history!

The first thing we need to note about the antichrist here is that we are told at verse 3 that it appeared as if one of its heads "had been slain," which when translated literally is 'slaughtered to death.' The word "slain" here is "Sphazo" in the original, which speaks of human life being taken. We then note that "his fatal wound was healed," where the word "fatal" is "Thanatos," which is the word used to speak of death, here having physical death in view. The word "wound" here is "Plege" in the original Greek, while the word "healed" is "Therapeuo," meaning to be restored to health. What we have here then at Revelation 13:3,12,14 is the antichrist appearing to have had a fatal blow that leads to physical death, and then was restored to health again, in that the antichrist appears to have been killed and then brought back to life!

The devil, the antichrist, and the false prophet being seen as but fallen angels!

In now knowing about the dragon as the devil; the beast from the sea as the antichrist; and the beast from the earth as the false prophet, we can now turn to Revelation 16:13,14, and note there what we are further told about these three evil characters, "[13] And I saw coming out of the mouth of the dragon (who is the devil) and out of the mouth of the beast (who is the antichrist as the first beast of Revelation 13:1) and out of the mouth of the false prophet (the second beast of Revelation 13:11), three unclean spirits like frogs; for they are SPIRITS OF DEMONS, performing signs, which go out to the kings of the whole world, to gather them together for the war of the great day of God, the Almighty."

In other words, what we are to grasp here from this is that since we know that the devil is a fallen angelic being, then the antichrist and the false prophet are also! In other words, now we know the true identity of the antichrist and the false prophet in that they are both fallen angelic beings, which are evil spirits or demons, now on earth in a male human body, carrying out the will of the devil during the last seven years remaining of the second age of time!

So while the devil remains unseen here, the antichrist is the visible political leader having the rule over the nations of the earth, while the false prophet is the visible religious leader under the authority of the antichrist, with both continuing to be under the direct authority and power of the devil. Let us remember here that angelic beings, because they are spirit beings, whether unfallen or fallen, always take on a human body when appearing visibly in the physical realm of earth. Therefore, this is the case for both the antichrist and the false prophet on earth during these seven years here!

The devil's attempt at counterfeiting what God does through His Son, The Lord Jesus Christ, by His Holy Spirit!

In now knowing the true identity of these two evil characters, let us now go on and see what the objectives are for the devil raising demons in male human form as the antichrist and the false prophet at this time in human history. And in order to discover that we need to be aware of what God's Son is about to do on earth, when He comes as part of the second stage of His second coming from Heaven to earth, which is at the end of the last seven years remaining of the second age of time, as is clear from Revelation 19:11-16. And let us remember here that the antichrist rules directly over the nations of the earth during the first three and half years and then is assisted by the false prophet in the last three and half years, as is clear from what we have seen from Revelation 13.

So what God's Son is about to do in His second stage of His second coming is to establish the Kingdom of Heaven here on earth, which was not accomplished during His first coming from Heaven to earth, which first coming God The Father instead used to bring redemption to a lost human race, through His death at the cross due the sins of mankind, before being buried to put those sins away, and then raised from the dead the third day, to be alive forevermore so as to provide His Father the basis by which He grants the forgiveness of sins and eternal life to all who believe in His Son during their time on earth!

And this still remains somewhat of a mystery until we grasp what God told us at Revelation 12:9 about the devil, namely that he "deceives the whole world..." with one way of his attempting to do this is through COUNTERFEITING what God does during the four ages of time, for the purpose of leading people astray from God to worship him instead of God! In other words, God created human beings, who were made in His likeness and image (noting Genesis 1:26), in order that they might worship Him. So the devil seeks to lead people to reject God and to worship him instead.

What is very important to realize here is that just as God is outworking an eternal plan in all that He does in time; the devil is likewise working from a plan for all he does in time, even though he is a created being, who had his beginning in time and has therefore not eternally existed. And just as God is working toward an end objective in all He does, which is to secure willing service from His human creation out of love for Him; likewise the devil is also working toward an end objective, which is to secure worship to himself from as many humans as he can, for both time and eternity.

What this means is that the devil needs to prevent human beings from coming to know God on the one hand, for then such will be worshipping God, if not all the time during time, then at least all of the time for all eternity. Then at the same time, since the devil's ultimate goal is to secure worship for himself, which he knows he will have from all unbelievers both during time and for all eternity, he attempts to thwart worship to God during time through introducing IDOLATRY into the human race!

It should not surprise us then to see God throughout His word try to steer human beings away from idol worship, so as not to fall into the sin of idolatry, noting for instance what God says in the very first of His Ten Commandments at Exodus 20:3-5, "[3] You shall have no other gods before Me. [4] You shall not make for yourself an idol (that is, a graven image), or any likeness of what is in heaven above or on the earth beneath or in the water under the earth. [5] You shall not worship them or serve them; for I, the Lord your God, am a jealous God, visiting the iniquity of the fathers on the children, on the third and the fourth generations of those who hate Me..."

What is important for us to remember here then is that idolatry is simply idol worship. Since an idol is something put forth as being an image of a supposed deity, then the worship of that idol is idolatry. What this means for our present purpose here is that whereas God tries to prevent human beings from worshipping idols, so as not to fall into the sin of idolatry; the devil on the other hand is doing all he can, with the help of his fallen angels, who are demons, including unbelievers of earth, to have as many human beings worship idols, and so fall into the sin of idolatry! We are to see that one of the devil's activities is to act not only as an antagonist to God, but also as a counterfeiter of all that God does. Well, we are seeing that here to the nth degree, in what the devil has the antichrist and the false prophet do on earth during the last seven years remaining of the second age of time!

And we are now to see that that during this seven years left of the second age of time, during which time the antichrist and the false prophet will be operating on earth under the devil's direct authority and power, the devil will be attempting to set up worldwide service and worship of himself here on earth! And so for our present purpose here, we are to see that the devil, as the dragon, is attempting to set up his kingdom on earth through a one world government under the antichrist, while at the same time attempting to secure service and worship for himself by means of these TRIUNE EVIL BEINGS AS COUNTERFEITS OF GOD THE FATHER, HIS SON, AND THE HOLY SPIRIT!

And so it is critical for us to see here that this evil trio here are attempting to counterfeit the Godhead, with the devil seeking to counterfeit The Father, Who is always invisible to human beings; with the antichrist seeking to counterfeit The Son of God, Christ, Who is always the visible representation of God to human beings; while the false prophet will seek to counterfeit The Holy Spirit. And so, just as The Father gave all power and authority into the hands of His precious Son (noting Matthew 28:18; John 3:35), Who represented God The Father while on earth (noting John 14:7-9; Hebrews 1:2,3), while The Holy Spirit sought to make The Son known (noting John 14:26; John 15:26; John 16:13-15); so too here at Revelation 13, we see the devil, as the dragon, giving his authority to the first beast, as the antichrist, who in the first three and half years left of the second age of time, will have all the power and authority of the devil; while the second beast will, in the last half of this seven year period, be seeking to make the antichrist known to human beings on earth!.

And so we see at Revelation 13:12,13 above that the second beast, as the false prophet, exercises all the authority of the first beast, who is the antichrist, and deceives all the unbelievers of earth through the signs that he does, so that God, in allowing this, is in effect saying to the human race in unbelief here, 'you refused to believe in Me, through believing in My Son while The Holy Spirit was on earth indwelling believers during this third age of time. Well, now that I have removed all believers of earth with the removal of The Holy Spirit to now begin the seven years of my wrath against you, then be deceived and believe in these evil counterfeits, namely worshiping the devil through the antichrist by way of the false prophet!' And just as God is about to establish His Kingdom on earth through His Son at the end of this seven year period, so too is the devil here seeking to establish his own counterfeit kingdom on earth, and have as many people in it to serve and worship him as he can!

Then we need to note that at Revelation 13:14, this second beast, as the false prophet, has the unbelievers of earth make an image of the first beast, which means that this image is man-made, which means it is an idol. Then we need to note that the second beast, as the false prophet, has everyone killed who will not worship this image of the first beast, who is the antichrist. And if it be asked here: Why have an image of the first beast? The answer is that the devil is here continuing to counterfeit all that God did through His precious Son, The Lord Jesus Christ, in the sense that just as God's Son died and then was raised to life again; and so the devil in his attempt to counterfeit this allows the antichrist, as the first beast, to also be killed with a sword, and since he is a demon and cannot die, but has only human appearance, and so the devil is able to have the antichrist, as a demon in male human form, "come to life" as it were.

And then just as God's Son returned to Heaven again and sent The Holy Spirit as His representative on earth, so too does the devil try to counterfeit this by now having the second beast, as the false prophet, represent both the devil and the antichrist on earth by having an image made of the first beast which can speak! We should not be skeptical here that such a thing can be done, especially when we consider that we presently are capable of producing holograms, which are three dimensional images of an actual person. In other words, a person can be projected on stage anywhere on earth, speaking to an audience, while not physically present, but just the holographic image being seen! And so, when we read at Revelation 13:15 here, "it was given him to give breath to the image of the beast," we are to see that the immediate source of this power was from the devil, who enabled the false prophet; although all of this was being allowed of God to serve His purpose in time, or else the enemy, the devil, would not have been allowed to do such a thing from himself.

And then, same as The Holy Spirit when He first came, was enabled of God The Father to have some believers on earth do supernatural signs to authenticate them as really being from God, then now we see the devil enable to second beast at Revelation 13:13 to also do supernatural signs on earth! But whereas God's supernatural signs were for the benefit of those who saw them, that they might believe in God and be saved; the devil on the other hand has the false prophet do these signs so as to deceive those on earth, so that they will not believe in God and be saved, therefore remaining part of his kingdom forever in hell, which this present earth becomes after the final judgment of time (noting 2 Peter 3:7 with Revelation 20:11-15)! So the devil is ever to be seen as not only counterfeiting God, but also seen to ever be working at cross purposes to what God is doing, so as to try to prevent God's plan of the ages of time from being carried out!

And then we see from Revelation 13:16,17 that the devil is not content with just having the second beast, as the false prophet, try to assure that only the image, as an idol, is worshipped in what he now has him do, as we now here see, "[16] And he causes all, the small and the great, and the rich and the poor, and the free men and the slaves, to be given a mark on their right hand or on their forehead, [17] and he provides that no one will be able to buy or to sell, except the one who has the mark, either the name of the beast or the number of his name."

What we see here in the words, "he causes all," is that the devil through the first beast, as the antichrist, by second beast, as the false prophet - because still attempting to counterfeit on earth how God works - will be forcing all human beings on earth "to be given a mark on their right hand or on their forehead," so that only those who have this mark, which only unbelievers will ever accept, will be given "either the name of the beast or the number of his name," by which they will then "be able to buy or sell" on earth!

And what should be obvious here is that the main commodity to be sold or bought would be food, since everyone needs to eat. And what is equally evident here is that this means that one of the things that the devil needs on earth is a cashless society. In other words, there needs to be a digital economy in place on earth in order for this to function, so as to be able to control the production, distribution, and selling of food all along the food chain.

What this also supposes is that there is a system of worldwide surveillance in place, where not only all the activities of cities can be monitored, but also all the remote areas of the earth, so as to prevent those who refuse the mark, because they are believers – which means they also refuse to worship the image of the beast – to move out to the open country somewhere so as to attempt to grow their own food. What this also supposes is that there is also a system in place to deal a deathly blow to any who try to escape, so as not to have the mark of the beast, which method of extermination of course already exists through all the drones presently in use to kill anyone at any moment's notice, day or night, in any weather condition, anywhere on earth!

What is critical to see here is that none of this applies to any believer presently on earth during this present third age, for all believers of earth will already have been removed from the earth at the first stage of the second coming of God's precious Son to end this present third age we are now in. This therefore means that only those who become believers during the seven years left of the second age of time are affected here, with the events now in view at Revelation 13:16,17 only taking place on earth during the second half of that seven year period, since it is the second beast, as the false prophet, who is exercising authority on earth at this time, who only does so during the second half of the seven years, as already noted above.

What should also be noted here is that in this second beast being identified as "the false prophet," would therefore indicate a religious figure, who would be the head of the apostate church on earth. This is also why this second beast was said to be "from the earth" and not "from the sea," as the first beast, who will be from one of the nations of the revived Roman empire, which is from one of the nations of present-day Europe (as we will see in the next chapter). In the case of the false prophet, he will not be a ruler of a nation, but rather a prominent religious figure on earth in one of the nations of earth, which will also be part of the revived Roman empire.

What this also means then relating to the eventual end of the antichrist, especially in relation to the antichrist incurring a fatal wound on one of its heads, which was then healed, is the fact that since the antichrist is a demon in male human form, and since demons cannot die, then this means that his body can incur as many wounds as anyone can give to it, but it will never die. This is why we see, for instance, the antichrist and the false prophet go directly to the fire of hell without going through physical death, as all human unbelievers do, at Revelation 19:20, where God tells us what the eventual end is for the antichrist and the false prophet, "And the beast (as the first one of Revelation 13:1, who is the antichrist) was seized, and with him the false prophet (who is the second beast of Revelation 13:11) performed the signs in his presence, by which he deceived those who had received the mark of the beast and those who worshiped his image; these two were THROWN ALIVE into the lake of fire which burns with brimstone," this being eternal hell.

And that is also why the devil, who is also a fallen angelic being and leader of all evil spirits, who are demons, later joins them there without going through physical death either, as we see at Revelation 20:10, "And the devil who deceived them was THROWN INTO THE LAKE OF FIRE and brimstone, where the beast and the false prophet are also; and they will be tormented day and night forever and ever," simply because angelic beings are not subject to physical death. Had the devil, the antichrist, and the false prophet been human beings, then they never would have gone directly to the lake of fire, which is hell, without first going through physical death, as all human beings in unbelief do, as God makes clear at Hebrews 9:27, "And inasmuch as it is appointed for men (in unbelief in all ages of time) TO DIE ONCE and after this comes judgment..."

And so that is why we read at Revelation 13:3 that one of the antichrist's heads was only "AS IF it had been slain," simply because it was impossible for the antichrist to die, same as God says at Acts 2:24 that it was impossible for His Son, The Lord Jesus Christ, to be held in the grip of death, since He too as The Son of God was an eternal spirit Being like His Father (noting John 4:24), which was why God The Father raised His Son from the dead three days later. This means that at Revelation 13:3 here, we again certainly have the antichrist trying to counterfeit God's Son! And in now knowing these truths, we now have a better grasp of what the true identity of the antichrist is; and what the objectives of the devil are in bringing the antichrist and the false prophet on the world scene in time!

"[20] The ram which you saw with the two horns represents the kings of Media and Persia.[21] The shaggy goat represents the kingdom of Greece, and the large horn that is between his eyes is the first king."

Daniel 8:20,21

CHAPTER THREE

/ Seeing from God's word at Daniel 2 and 9 that the antichrist does indeed arise out of a revived Roman Empire, which is present day Europe!

God's disclosure of there being four world empires of mankind on earth followed by the establishment of the Kingdom of His own dear Son, before time ends!

The place to begin is with the book of Daniel in God's word, where God discloses at Daniel chapter 2 that during the ages of time there will be FOUR WORLD EMPIRES that will arise before He destroys these four world empires with the coming of HIS OWN WORLD EMPIRE, which will be from Heaven and will have His Son as King over the nations of the earth!

In order to see this here, let us note what we read at Daniel 2:31-45, where we have the prophet Daniel briefly give Nebuchadnezzar, who is the king of Babylon and is to be the ruler of the first of these four world empires, what his dream was and what is God's interpretation of that dream, there now reading, with capitalization added as a help, "[31] "You, O king, were looking and behold, there was A SINGLE GREAT STATUE; that statue, which was large and of extraordinary splendor, was standing in front of you, and its appearance was awesome. [32] THE HEAD OF THE STATUE WAS MADE OF FINE GOLD, ITS BREAST AND ITS ARMS OF SILVER, ITS BELLY AND ITS THIGHS OF BRONZE, [33] ITS LEGS OF IRON, ITS FEET PARTLY OF IRON AND PARTLY OF CLAY. [34] You continued looking until A STONE WAS CUT OUT WITHOUTH HANDS, AND IT STRUCK

41

THE STATUE ON ITS FEET OF IRON AND CLAY AND CRUSHED THEM. [35] Then the iron, the clay, the bronze, the silver and the gold were crushed all at the same time and became like chaff from the summer threshing floors; and the wind carried them away so that not a trace of them was found. But the stone that struck the statue became a great mountain and filled the whole earth. [36] THIS WAS THE DREAM, NOW WE WILL TELL ITS INTERPRETATION before the king. [37] YOU, O KING, ARE THE KING OF KINGS, TO WHOM THE GOD OF HEAVEN HAS GIVEN THE KINGDOM, the power, the strength and the glory; [38] and wherever the sons of men dwell, or the beasts of the field, or the birds of the sky, He has given them into your hand and has caused you to rule over them all. YOU ARE THE HEAD OF GOLD. [39] AFTER YOU THERE WILL ARISE ANOTHER KINGDOM INFERIOR TO YOU, THEN ANOTHER THIRD KINGDOM OF BRONZE, WHICH WILL RULE OVER ALL THE EARTH.[40] THEN THERE WILL BE A FOURTH KINGDOM AS STRONG AS IRON; inasmuch as iron crushes and shatters all things, so, like iron that breaks in pieces, IT WILL CRUSH AND BREAK ALL THESE IN PIECES. [41] In that you saw the feet and toes, partly of potter's clay and partly of iron, it will be a divided kingdom; but it will have in it the toughness of iron, inasmuch as you saw the iron mixed with common clay. [42] As the toes of the feet were partly of iron and partly of pottery, so some of the kingdom will be strong and part of it will be brittle. [43] And in that you saw the iron mixed with common clay, they will combine with one another in the seed of men; but they will not adhere to one another, even as iron does not combine with pottery. [44] IN THE DAYS OF THOSE KINGS THE GOD OF HEAVEN WILL SET UP A KINGDOM WHICH WILL NEVER BE DESTROYED, AND THAT KINGDOM will not be left for another people; it WILL CRUSH AND PUT AN END TO ALL THESE KINGDOMS, BUT IT WILL ITSELF ENDURE FOREVER. [45] Inasmuch as you saw that a stone was cut out of the mountain without hands and that it crushed the iron, the bronze, the clay, the silver and the gold, THE GREAT GOD HAS MADE KNOWN TO THE KING WHAT WILL TAKE PLACE IN THE FUTURE; so the dream is true and its interpretation is trustworthy."

What is important to notice here is that at Daniel 2:39, Nebuchadnezzar, king of Babylon, is told, "After you there will arise another kingdom," which therefore means that what we read at Daniel 2:37,38 concerns Nebuchadnezzar as also ruling over a kingdom as "the head of gold" of the statue in view at Daniel 2:31-33. And what is also very important to grasp here is that based on the description that is given of "the kingdom" that Nebuchadnezzar will rule over as the head of gold is the fact that this is a kingdom that is over the whole of the known world. In other words, 'a world empire' is what Nebuchadnezzar had been granted by God here, as would also be true in regards to each of the subsequent three kingdoms mentioned here!

And then we note at Daniel 2:37 that Nebuchadnezzar is referred to as "the king of kings," as one who has "the power, the strength and the glory," which we see was all given by "the God of heaven," which we must see here means God is not only Himself higher and greater than all this, since He is uncreated and eternal in contrast to mankind; but is also in full control of this, as part of His own original creation!

We know the whole earth is here in view due to being told at verse 38, "wherever the sons of men dwell, or the beasts of the field, or the birds of the sky, He has given them into your hand and has caused you to rule over them all." Therefore, it is clear that a worldwide kingdom of mankind is in view in the head of gold, which begins in the days of Nebuchadnezzar, who is king of Babylon. What this further means then is that the first world empire is a Babylonian one, and that in time there will be three other such world empires of men.

Then when Nebuchadnezzar is told at Daniel 2:39 that after him "there will arise another kingdom inferior to you," we are to note that the inferiority is also reflected in the metal used to describe each subsequent kingdom, since gold, which is used to describe the Babylonian kingdom, is more valuable and desirable than silver, which is used to describe the next kingdom, or world empire; with the next kingdom, or third world empire, that of bronze, will therefore be even more inferior, just as bronze has lesser value and desirability than silver. And again at the end of Daniel 2:39 here, we see that the kingdoms in view are indeed world-encompassing in the words, "will rule over all the earth."

What is then important to note from Daniel 2:40-43 is that here we have the mention of a fourth kingdom of men, or world empire, which in comparison to the second and third kingdoms, which each took less than a verse of space to mention, now takes four full verses; which must mean that we are to pay special attention to this fourth kingdom of mankind! And what is also important to notice here from Daniel 2:40 is that this fourth kingdom begins strong, because the legs are all of iron, and will crush and break the previous kingdom "in pieces... like iron that breaks in pieces." But as time goes on that fourth kingdom will become a divided kingdom, "in that you saw the feet and toes, partly of potter's clay and partly of iron."

What is therefore also very important to notice here is that as we move from the head to the feet and toes of the statue, we are in fact MOVING FORWARD IN TIME, so that each of these four kingdoms of men come one after the other in human history on earth. What is also interesting to notice is that the fourth kingdom is not pictured as divided by the fact of having two legs of iron, but rather is shown in the future be a divided kingdom based on having the iron "mixed with common clay" in the feet of the statue. What this further means is that part of the kingdom will still have a certain measure of strength, while part of the kingdom will nevertheless be "brittle," that is, will be weaker.

Then what is critical here is knowing the proper meaning of Daniel 2:43, especially the words "they will combine with one another in the seed of men; but they will not adhere to one another." One thing which appears clear, based on the mention of iron mixed with clay at both the beginning and end of this verse is that the fourth kingdom is very much still in view here, but now seen further in history as time progresses. Therefore, the questions that become paramount in finding answers to are: What does "they will combine with one another in the seed of men" mean? And what does "they will not adhere to one another" mean?

The word "combine" here is "Arab" in the original, also meaning 'to mix.' For instance, the word "mixed" at both Daniel 2:41 and Daniel 2:43 here is the word "Arab." Then we note that the word "seed" is "Zera" in the original Aramaic, having reference here – because followed by the word "men" – to offspring or descendants of men. Then we note that the word "adhere" is "Debeq" in the original, meaning 'to cling.'

What this therefore means is that the fourth kingdom will go on existing from its inception in the history of mankind until such time as God Himself destroys it at some point in the future. And so, that fourth kingdom will still exist among men, in that the nations making up the kingdom will still exist, but it will not be seen as being a worldwide kingdom. In other words, this fourth kingdom WILL NOT BE SEEN AT THAT TIME IN THE FUTURE AS RULING OVER THE WHOLE EARTH, even though the various nations within it will still exist. We will come back to talk about this fourth kingdom here as soon as we finish talking about the fifth kingdom, which is not of men, at Daniel 2:44.

And so, what is then critical for us to grasp from Daniel 2:44 is that when we are told here, "In the days of those kings," we are to realize that this is now referring to the days of the fourth kingdom as it is presented at Daniel 2:43, namely, as seen here at the time of the future; in the days when the nations within the kingdom still exist, but the kingdom itself is no longer ruling over the whole earth. And what will occur at that time is that "The God of Heaven will set up a Kingdom, which will never be destroyed, (in that it will be eternal), and that Kingdom will not be left for another people (that is, it will not be a succession to the previous kingdoms of men); it will crush and put an end to all these kingdoms (in reference to the four kingdoms of men seen typified by the statue here at Daniel 2), but it will itself endure forever."

And since we then see from Daniel 2:45 that this fifth Kingdom, which is of God and not of men, will put an end to all the previous kingdoms, or world-encompassing empires of men; this means then that the four kingdoms of men that we have had in view in the various component parts of the statue runs its course in history from the time of the Babylonian empire until the fifth kingdom is set up in the future! And the obvious question which arises here is: What is this fifth Kingdom in reference to that we clearly see here is from God?

The only answer that is possible here, based on what God has made known in His word regarding His Kingdom during the four ages of time, is that this is a reference to the Kingdom which is setup over the whole earth and over which God's Son, The Lord Jesus Christ, will rule on His return to the earth at the time of the second stage of His second coming from Heaven to earth, which is at the end of the last seven years left of the second age of time, which will run its course after the present third age has ended. That fifth Kingdom is to be seen then as being the "Kingdom of Heaven" in view in Matthew's gospel account, which could not be established on earth at the first coming from Heaven to earth of God's Son, The Lord Jesus Christ, because He was rejected by the nation of Israel as their King, due to the unbelief of the nation, as represented by its leadership.

What also needs to be grasped here is that this fifth Kingdom is the ONLY Kingdom that God prophesied about in His word as coming from the genealogy of David and being eternal, noting what David was told by God through the prophet Nathan at 1 Chronicles 17:10b-14, "[10b] Moreover, I tell you that the Lord will build a house for you (David). [11] When your days are fulfilled that you must go to be with your fathers, that I will set up one of your descendants after you, who will be of your sons; and I will establish his kingdom. [12] He shall build for Me a house, and I will establish his throne forever. [13] I will be his father and he shall be My son; and I will not take My lovingkindness away from him, as I took it from him who was before you (that is, Saul). [14] But I will settle him in My house and in My kingdom forever, and his throne shall be established forever." "

And so we need to grasp here that the "kingdom" in view at 1 Chronicles 17:11 is the same "kingdom" as is in view at Daniel 2:44, the only exception being that at 1 Chronicles 17 the word "kingdom" is in Hebrew; while at Daniel 2:44, the word "kingdom" is in Aramaic. And this is also to be seen as being the same kingdom that God has in view at Luke 1:31-33, relating again to God's Son, The Lord Jesus Christ, "[31] And behold, you will conceive in your womb and bear a son, and you shall name Him Jesus. [32] He will be great and will be called the Son of the Most High; and the Lord God will give Him the throne of His father David; [33] and He will reign over the house of Jacob forever, and His kingdom will have no end." Let us note that what God says in the last part of verse 33 here, namely that "His kingdom will have no end" is exactly what God says at the end of Daniel 2:44 in the words "it will itself endure forever."

What also needs to be noticed as an aside here is that when God talks to David at 1 Chronicles 17:14 above about "My kingdom," He is there talking about the same "Kingdom of Heaven," which His precious Son, The Lord Jesus Christ, will have ruled over during the duration of the fourth age of time, which will be of a thousand year duration, which He then hands over to His precious Father, which then becomes the "Kingdom of The Father," from that point on and into eternity, noting here for instance what we read at 1 Corinthians 15:24,25, "[24] then comes the end (of the fourth age), when He (The Son of God) hands over the kingdom (of Heaven that He has been ruling over on earth for the duration of the fourth age) to the God and Father, when He has abolished all rule and all authority and power. [25] For He (The Son of God, The Lord Jesus Christ) must reign until He has put all His enemies under His feet." The same Kingdom as at Daniel 2:44 is again also in view in the parable of the tares in the field at Matthew 13:36-43.

Therefore, as already mentioned above, since this fifth Kingdom, which is solely of God, will not be established on earth until the second stage of the second coming from Heaven to earth of God's Son, The Lord Jesus Christ, then this means that the four kingdoms of men, starting with Nebuchadnezzar, and as seen in the component parts of the statue of Daniel 2, must run their course on earth until that time. In other words, the fourth kingdom, which is of men, is still in existence on earth during the present third age and will be until the fifth kingdom comes, which is of God, which is not until approximately seven years after the end of the present third age of time.

But what is also of great importance for us here is that since God identified Nebuchadnezzar as the head of gold for us at Daniel 2:37,38, in the interpretation of the dream that He gave through His servant Daniel, then this means that God is again making a connection here between the history which He here gives in His word and what mankind has discovered in history through archeology. In other words, since the Babylonian empire is the first world-encompassing empire of men on earth, which God identifies here, then this means that the second world empire of men, shown by the two arms of silver, is the earthly kingdom of Media and Persia, which we know from extra-Biblical history followed it! But more importantly, God actually tells us later at Daniel 8:20 that the next world empire after that of the Babylonians is that of Media and Persia!

Then similarly, the third, shown by the belly and thighs of bronze is the world empire that was ruled by Greece, which we again know from extra-Biblical sources and archeology followed the world encompassing empire of Media-Persia. And again, God does not leave us to guess about these things since at Daniel 8:21 God Himself identifies the third world empire as being ruled by Greece! This leaves just one world empire to identify, which is the fourth empire, shown by the legs of iron and feet partly of iron and partly of clay, which although never mentioned by God by name in the book of Daniel, we know for sure from extra-Biblical sources and archeology that this cannot be anything else but that of Rome!

And since Rome was that fourth world empire that came into existence, and which still exists in our day, it is critical for us to grasp that since that original Roman Empire consisted of the nations that eventually became Europe, then this means that the Roman empire seen in the last days by God at Daniel 2:44 in the words, "In the days of those kings," as when that fifth kingdom, which is God's own Kingdom of Heaven is being established on earth, that God has in view at that time a revived form of the Roman empire of old, which still consists of the nations of present day Europe!

At Daniel 2:28, God had made known to Nebuchadnezzar through Daniel that the vision concerned mysteries which would take place "in the latter days," which is literally 'in the end of days.' And what God had in view by this statement is that at the time of Daniel, they were then in the second age of time, which was the age in which God was dealing with the nations of the earth through the believers of the nation of Israel. And so, the "latter days," or 'the end of days,' refers to the end of that second age of time!

What this means then, and this is important to grasp here, is that the reference by God at Daniel 2:44 in saying "In the days of those kings" is speaking of when the last seven years resumes again after the end of the present third age, with God now completing that seven years in this time of tribulation on earth, which God has in view in His word from Revelation 6:1 to Revelation 19:21, which is when the fourth kingdom, consisting of the nations of Europe of today, will again be in view in God's eternal plan for the earth. This is when God will then destroy this fourth kingdom at the end of that seven year period with the coming to earth of God's Son again, The Lord Jesus Christ, to now establish the Kingdom of Heaven over the earth, which He will then rule over during the fourth age of time. At Revelation 21:10 to Revelation 22:5, we see the city coming down from God in Heaven as being where God's Son will be residing during the fourth age, which has a duration of one thousand years.

God's disclosure of 70 weeks in the history of the nation of Israel at Daniel 9:24-27, where we will see three things, one that there is 69 weeks from the issuing of the decree to rebuild Jerusalem until the death of His Son at the cross, which then leaves one week for later in history; two, where we will also now see the antichrist coming out of a revived Roman Empire, which is present day Europe; and three, where we will also see that there is indeed seven years left to run its course of the second age of time!

And so, as we will now see from what God says at Daniel 9:24-27, we have here one of the most important prophecies in all the word of God, which needs to be understood by anyone wishing to have an understanding of God's later prophecies, and so there reading, "[24] Seventy weeks have been decreed for your people and your holy city, to finish the transgression, to make an end of sin, to make atonement for iniquity, to bring in everlasting righteousness, to seal up vision and prophecy and to anoint the most holy place. [25] So you are to know and discern that from the issuing of a decree to restore and rebuild Jerusalem until Messiah the Prince there will be seven weeks and sixty-two weeks; it will be built again, with plaza and moat, even in times of distress. [26] Then after the sixty-two weeks the Messiah will be cut off and have nothing, and the people of the prince who is to come will destroy the city and the sanctuary. And its end *will come* with a flood; even to the end there will be war; desolations are determined. [27] And he will make a firm covenant with the many for one week, but in the middle of the week he will put a stop to sacrifice and grain offering; and on the wing of abominations will come one who makes desolate, even until a complete destruction, one that is decreed, is poured out on the one who makes desolate."

The first truth we need to grasp here is that this prophecy concerns "your people and your holy city." And since Daniel was Jewish, being of the tribe of Judah (noting Daniel 1:6), then it is clear that the prophecy we read at verses 9:24-27 concerns the nation of Israel and its capital, Jerusalem, which is the "holy city" in view here (noting Nehemiah 11:1). Then a second very important truth to grasp is that in God saying here, "Seventy weeks have been decreed," this is to be seen as being God Who so decrees, with the 70 weeks needing to be seen as 70 times 7 years, or 490 years, so that a "week" here is not a literal week, but rather speaks of seven years!

One way we know this for certain is based on what we read at verse 9:25, where we are told, "from the issuing of a decree to restore and rebuild Jerusalem until Messiah the Prince there will be seven weeks and sixty-two weeks...," in other words, 69 weeks. If the 69 weeks here were literal weeks, then that would mean there would be 69 times 7 days equals 483 days for what we read in this verse to take place, which we know for sure is an utter impossibility, as we will see. Therefore, the 70 weeks must mean 70 times 7 years, or 490 years, so that 69 weeks equals 483 years, with one week, or seven years, then remaining to see the prophecy totally fulfilled!

Then a third very important truth to grasp before looking in detail at what takes place within those 490 years is noting that at verse 9:25 we are given the STARTING POINT of the prophecy, which is "from the issuing of a decree to restore and rebuild Jerusalem," and also the END POINT of the 69th week of the prophecy, which is "until Messiah the Prince," being here in reference to when God's precious Son comes from Heaven to earth in human flesh as The Lord Jesus Christ, which it is important to see is not in reference to the time of His virgin birth on earth, nor of when He started His public ministry, but rather, when God's precious Son, The Lord Jesus Christ, died on the cross, indicated here at verse 9:26 as "the Messiah will be cut off."

We further note that the words "cut off" here speak of His physical death, noting Genesis 7:20-22 with Genesis 9:11; and also noting what God tells us regarding His Son, as The Messiah, at Isaiah 53:8, "By oppression and judgment He was taken away; and as for His generation, who considered that He was cut off out of the land of the living for the transgression of my people, to whom the stroke was due?" Even though two different Hebrew words are used for the words "cut off," nevertheless both references are indicating physical death here. What this means then is that the END POINT for the 69th week of the prophecy is when the death of God's precious Son, The Lord Jesus Christ, occurred in time!

Then if one were to calculate the number of days from this start point of when the decree was given to end point at the death of God's precious Son, this would be 69 weeks times 7 years, which equals 483 years. And since one year is made up of 12 months of 30 days each in the Jewish calendar, which is what must be used here, then we have 360 days per year times 483 years equals 173, 880 days. And if we were to work backwards from when the death of God's precious Son occurred, which was in 33 AD, then 483 years prior to this would bring us to approximately 449 BC, as when the decree would have been issued by Artaxerxes in the 20th year of his reign (as we will see below).

Then a fourth critical truth to be aware of is that the starting point of the prophecy "from the issuing of a decree to restore and rebuild Jerusalem," was NOT the decree issued by Cyrus in his first year, which was in 516 BC, which we see at Ezra 1:1-5, which was a decree issued solely for the rebuilding of the temple in Jerusalem, and not the city of Jerusalem itself. At Ezra 4, we see the enemies of the land, who were opposed to the Jews rebuilding the temple, write to Artaxerxes, who was over the whole empire of Media and Persia at the time, and made the false accusation that that Jews were actually rebuilding the city itself. This resulted in the building of the temple being stopped from that point until many years later, with God having to raise the prophets Haggai and Zechariah, as we see at Ezra 5:1, to encourage the people to finish building the temple, which was then not completed until Darius' sixth year of his reign, which is after he had begun to rule over the whole of the Media-Persia empire, noting Ezra 6:15.

And what should also be mentioned here is that the Artaxerxes mentioned at Ezra 4:7 and Ezra 7:1, and following, is NOT the same Artaxerxes as mentioned at Nehemiah 2:1, who is the one who now has a key role in the prophecy of Daniel 9:24-27, as especially relating to its starting point, as we will now see. What this means then is that the decree, which is the starting point for God's prophecy through Daniel at verses 9:24-27, is the one we read about at Nehemiah 2:1-8, with the specific year and month being given at verse 2:1, with capitalization and notes in brackets added as a help, "[1] And it came about in the month Nisan, in the twentieth year of King Artaxerxes, that wine was before him, and I (Nehemiah) took up the wine and gave it to the king. Now I had not been sad in his presence. [2] So the king said to me, "Why is your face sad though you are not sick? This is nothing but sadness of heart." Then I was very much afraid. [3] I said to the king, "Let the king live forever. Why should my face not be sad when the CITY, the place of my fathers' tombs, lies desolate and its gates have been consumed by fire?" [4] Then the king said to me, "What would you request?" So I prayed to the God of heaven. [5] I said to the king, "If it please the king, and if your servant has found favor before you, send me to Judah, to the CITY of my fathers' tombs, THAT I MAY REBUILD IT." [6] Then the king said to me, the queen sitting beside him, "How long will your journey be, and when will you return?" So IT PLEASED THE KING TO SEND ME, and I gave him a definite time. [7] And I said to the king, "If it please the king, LET LETTERS BE GIVEN ME for the governors of the provinces beyond the River, that they may allow me to pass through until I come to Judah, [8] AND A LETTER to Asaph the keeper of the king's forest, that he may give me timber to make beams for the gates of the fortress which is by the temple, for the wall of THE CITY and for the house to which I will go." And THE KING GRANTED THEM TO ME because the good hand of my God was on me."

Therefore, the starting point for the 490 years of the prophecy at Daniel 9:24-27 is the month of Nisan – which was the first month of the Jewish calendar AFTER the exile (noting Esther 3:7), which BEFORE the exile had been the month of Abib (noting Exodus 12:2 with 13:4) – in the 20th year of the reign of king Artaxerxes! This Artaxerxes here was king of Persia at this time, which meant that he was over the whole of the Media-Persia empire, which was sometimes referred to as simply 'Persia,' with its capital at Susa (noting Nehemiah 1:1). And we further note from Nehemiah 2:3 and 2:5 that it was the city of Jerusalem that Nehemiah asks Artaxerxes to go and rebuild.

And as background here, we can note from Nehemiah 1:1-3 that Nehemiah, while in the capital Susa of the Media-Persia empire, hears from his brother Hanani, and some other men who had just come from Judah, that "The remnant there in the province who survived the captivity are in great distress and reproach, and the wall of Jerusalem is broken down and its gates are burned with fire." We then note from Nehemiah 1:4 that Nehemiah is greatly exercised at hearing this news so that he "wept and mourned for days," and "was fasting and praying before The God of heaven." It is important for us to grasp that this exercise in Nehemiah is from God, because it was His desire to use Nehemiah personally to do something about this situation!

And so from Nehemiah 1:5-11, we have a record of Nehemiah's prayer, as what he was led of God to pray. And what we further need to grasp here is that when God leads us to pray for something, this means that this is the area that God's own heart is burdened about, with God then alleviating that burden by sharing it with us, burdening us with it also, and then by giving us the desire to be involved in dealing with it so as to alleviate it! What this means then is that there is no coincidence here to the short statement at the end of Nehemiah 1:11, "Now I was the cupbearer to the king," for as cupbearer, Nehemiah had daily access to the king. And so, as a result of this, we have what we have noted above at Nehemiah 2:1-8 then occur, where Nehemiah is sent to Jerusalem to help rebuild the wall around Jerusalem so that the city can be rebuilt, all in the will of God!

And in now continuing with our look at God's prophecy of Daniel 9:24-27, we see at Daniel 9:24 that God says, "Seventy weeks have been decreed for your people and your holy city, to…," with God then going on to mention six things that specifically takes place within the 70 weeks, that is, the 490 years of the prophecy, which are: 1) to finish the transgression, 2) to make an end of sin, 3) to make atonement for iniquity, 4) to bring in everlasting righteousness, 5) to seal up vision and prophecy and 6) to anoint the most holy place;" keeping in mind that all of this is in relation to the nation of Israel and its capital, Jerusalem, which are in view in the words "your people and your holy city."

In now looking at this in detail, we note that during this period of time, namely the seventy weeks, Israel will "finish the transgression," with the word "finish" being to bring to an end, that is, to completion; while the word "transgression" here speaks of rebellion, with the basic idea being of a breach of relationship between two parties; in this present case that being between the nation of Israel and God. So what God is saying here is that by the time these seventy weeks have passed, the nation of Israel will no longer be in rebellion against God, which we must realize here has been the spiritual condition of the nation of Israel from its beginning as a nation, which is from the time that Israel came out of Egypt under Moses. But by the time the full seventy weeks are completed, Israel's rebellion against God will have ended.

Then secondly, we note that God next points out that during this period of time of the seventy weeks, Israel as a nation will "make an end of sin." The word "sin" here has Israel's disobedience in view as a nation. In other words, during its history, Israel has not only been in rebellion against God and His word to them, but has also been in disobedience, which is always a sure sign of one being in unbelief, that is, of one not having a personal relationship with God in salvation. So what God is making known here is that by the time the seventy weeks are up, the nation of Israel will no longer be in unbelief, due to God bringing salvation to the nation of Israel, as we note below!

What this means then is that when the 70th week is complete, which is when God's Son comes from Heaven to earth again, which is at the time of the second stage of His second coming at the end of the seven years remaining of the second age of time, transgression and sin will be done with, since now all unbelievers of earth will have died, leaving only the elect (that is, those chosen of God for salvation) of the nation of Israel and the other nations of the earth, who will be alive at that time to receive their King and to serve Him willingly out of love for Him during the 1000 year duration of His reign over the earth during the fourth age of time.

Two verses which we can note in regards to what has just been said, specifically in relation to the nation of Israel, since they are the ones in view at Daniel 9:24, is what we read at Romans 11:26,,27, "[26] and so all Israel (the elect, as those chosen of God from the nation of Israel to receive salvation at this time) will be saved; just as it is written, "The Deliverer will come from Zion, He will remove ungodliness from Jacob." [27] This is My covenant with them, when I take away their sins." The "Deliverer" in view here is God's Son, The Lord Jesus Christ.

Then the third truth that God mentions at Daniel 9:24, as to what takes place within the 70 weeks, or 490 years, is "to make atonement for iniquity," which here refers to the death of God's own precious Son, The Lord Jesus Christ, which takes place at the end of the 69th week of the prophecy, as we will see again when we look at Daniel 9:25. The critical truth to grasp here is that the word "atonement" means to 'make reconciliation,' in terms of bringing two parties together again; in this case making provision to bring the sinner into a right relationship with God (Who is Holy, that is, without sin), due to the barrier caused by the sins of the sinner having been removed in the death of God's precious Son on the cross on behalf of sinners.

It is important to see that it is God Who provides that atonement through His Son. We can note here in this regard what God tells us from His word at 1 Timothy 2:5,6, "[5] For there is one God, and one mediator also between God and men, the man Christ Jesus, who gave Himself as a ransom for all, the testimony given at the proper time." And let us keep in mind that although God's Son died for the sins of the whole of the human race, nevertheless here at Daniel 9:24, God applies this in relation to the nation of Israel, as what will happen during this seventy week period, simply due to the nation of Israel being a representative nation during the second age of time, with this seventy weeks falling within that time period of the second age, when God was dealing with the nations of the earth through the believers of the nation of Israel.

In other words, all nations are here included in the nation of Israel as a representative nation. Just as Adam and Eve were real people, but representative of the whole human race, in that God knew that what these two did in sinning against God, any other two human beings would have done the same had they been in their place in the garden of Eden. And so, similarly with the nation of Israel as a representative nation, God knew that what this one nation does throughout its history, any other nation would have likewise done had it been chosen as a representative nation instead of Israel!

And what is also critical to grasp is that although atonement for the sins of mankind has been fully provided by the death of God's Son, so that He could say at John 19:30, when at the point of dying in the place of a sinful human race while hanging on the cross, "It is finished," relating to all that was to be fulfilled at His first coming from Heaven to earth, with the central work being atonement; nevertheless, what we are to see here is that if God's Son, The Lord Jesus Christ, had merely died and remained in the grave like any other corpse, then His death on behalf of a sinful human race would not have accomplished anything! In other words, God's Son, The Lord Jesus Christ, also needed to be raised from the dead in order to be alive forevermore, since it is through the death AND resurrection from the dead of The Son of God on one's behalf that the sinner who believes in Him now has the forgiveness of sins AND eternal life with God in salvation!

And so that is why that immediately after the mention of "to make atonement for iniquity," we then read the fourth truth at Daniel 9:24, "to bring in everlasting righteousness," which we are now to realize is a reference to God's own righteous life, or righteousness, which comes, along with the forgiveness of all of one's sins ever committed against God, the moment any sinner turns to God and believes the gospel, which is the good news that God has made known to mankind regarding His Son, The Lord Jesus Christ, noting here what God makes known at 1 Corinthians 15:1-4, "[1] Now I make known to you, brethren, THE GOSPEL which I preached to you, which also you received, in which also you stand, [2] BY WHICH ALSO YOU ARE SAVED, if you hold fast the word which I preached to you, unless you BELIEVED in vain. [3] For I delivered to you as of first importance what I also received, that CHRIST DIED FOR OUR SINS (the atonement) according to the Scriptures, [4] and that He was buried, and that HE WAS RAISED ON THE THIRD DAY (the bringing in of everlasting righteousness) according to the Scriptures..."

How important that we see that the atonement provided cannot be separated from the bringing in of God's righteousness, which God's Son brought to mankind through His resurrection from the dead the third day, as what also takes place within that seventy week period! Without The Son of God being alive forevermore, God's righteousness, which is His righteous life or eternal life, could not be imparted to a believer, since it is through The Son by The Holy Spirit that this life ever comes to the believer, that being any person who believes in Him as a work of God's grace and power alone!

It is important to remember and keep in mind here that the death at the cross of God's precious Son on behalf of a sinful human race was to make the provision for the removal of our sins, while His resurrection from the dead the third day was to make provision for a sinful mankind to receive God's own eternal life, or righteousness. But that forgiveness of sins and eternal life, although provided in the death and resurrection from the dead of God's Son, is only applied to a sinner's life by God when a sinner turns from sin to God (which is repentance) to believe the gospel, as to what God's Son has done on behalf of a sinful human race, namely His death for sins, His burial to put those sins away, and His resurrection from the dead the third day, so as to be eternally alive for God to impart one that eternal life through Him!

Any sinner who refuses to come to God and dies in one's unbelief will, after physical death, be raised from the dead by God to be judged for one's sins committed while on earth, which one refused to come to God to confess, and now one will suffer the consequence, which is eternal separation from God forever! There are only two places possible after physical death. Either one believes in God during one's stay on earth before death, and so receives the forgiveness of sins and eternal life now so as to go to Heaven after death; or else one refuses to believe, so that after physical death, one is cast by God into the lake of fire forever, which is an eternal hell, which is the judgment of God for refusing to accept God's free gift of His Son and His work on one's behalf during one's stay on earth.

Then the fifth truth we are further told at Daniel 9:24, as what also takes place within the seventy weeks, or 490 years, is "to seal up vision and prophecy" (literally 'prophet'). The word "vision" and the word "prophecy" (that is, 'prophet'), could also have been expressed as 'prophetic vision,' with both relating to God's spokesman, who is in view here in these two words, as one through whom God spoke during the second age of time.

Then the words "seal up," which is really one word in the original, is being used here in a metaphorical way (that is, as applying a name or descriptive term to an object to which it is not literally applicable). And to help us understand what God means by "seal up" in relation to "vision and prophecy," let us look at how God uses the word at Isaiah 29:11, where we read, "The entire vision will be to you like the words of a sealed book, which when they give it to the one who is literate, saying, "Please read this," he will say, "I cannot, for it is sealed." And so, at Daniel 9:24, God is saying that the prophetic visions of the prophets will be sealed, in terms of not being understood by the nation of Israel, due to being in unbelief, until that time near the end of the seventieth week, when God saves those who are elect of Him (that is, chosen of Him for salvation), who are still alive. They will at that time have a clear understanding of the prophetic visions, so that they will no longer be sealed!

Then we note that the sixth and final truth mentioned at Daniel 9:24, as relating to what takes place within the 70 weeks, or 490 years, is "to anoint the most holy *place*," with the word "place" here being an added word by the translators from Hebrew to English. And before we look at the words "most holy," let us note that the word "anoint" is "Mashah" in the original Hebrew, which has in view the induction into a ceremonial office, an action which involved the pouring of oil upon the head of an individual. So we see for instance at Leviticus 8:12 that Aaron was anointed as high priest in this way, "Then he poured some of the anointing oil on Aaron's head and anointed (Mashah) him, to consecrate him." The one so anointed would henceforth be consecrated to God, that is, would be set apart for God's service only.

Further on at 1 Samuel 16:13, we see that David was similarly anointed, but now as king, as we there read, "Then Samuel took the horn of oil and anointed (Mashah) him in the midst of his brothers; and the Spirit of the Lord came mightily upon David from that day forward..." And then at 1 Kings 19:16, we see that not only a high priest and a king were so anointed, but also a prophet, as we there read, "and Jehu the son of Nimshi you shall anoint (Mashah) king over Israel; and Elisha the son of Shaphat of Abel-meholah you shall anoint (Mashah) as prophet in your place."

The significance of seeing individuals being anointed to the offices of high priest, king, and prophet in the Old Testament is because when God's own precious Son later came from Heaven to earth to take on our humanity in the innocence of Adam as born of a virgin, He too was anointed of God by The Holy Spirit and will in time and forever hold these three offices of High Priest, Prophet, and King!

What needs to be observed here is that while God's Son, The Lord Jesus Christ, was anointed into the offices of High Priest and Prophet at His first coming from Heaven to earth, as we see in the New Testament; however, He was never anointed as King due to the nation of Israel being in unbelief, and so they rejected Him as King over the nation of Israel. What this means is that God's Son will not be anointed as King over the nation of Israel until the end of the 70 weeks or 490 years, when the elect of the nation of Israel, will do so at that time, once they have come to know God in salvation.

And so at Daniel 9:24, when God says "to anoint the most holy," leaving out the word "place," we see that the words "most holy" are one word in the original Hebrew, that being "Qodesh," which speaks of the essential nature of that which is set apart by God as sacred and therefore distinct from the common or profane. And in this case, it refers not to a place, but rather to a Person!

To see this here, let us look at 1 Chronicles 23:13, where we read, "The sons of Amram were Aaron and Moses. And AARON WAS SET APART TO SANCTIFY HIM AS MOST HOLY (Qodesh), he and his sons forever, to burn incense before the Lord, to minister to Him and to bless in His name forever." Here we see that Aaron, who had been anointed of God as high priest, is referred to as "most holy" (Qodesh), as one set apart for God's service. So that is why it is really unfortunate that the translators added the word "place" here, because this leads the reader to think of a place, whereas God is really speaking of a Person!

And so, we are to see that at Daniel 9:24 the "most holy" in view here is a reference to God's Son, The Lord Jesus Christ! And before we speak further on this, let us notice that after David had been anointed as king with oil by Samuel at 1 Samuel 16:13, as we have seen, nevertheless, it was not until after Saul had been removed by God from being king that David became king, first just over Judah, as we see at 2 Samuel 2:4, and it was not until much later before David was made king over the northern kingdom of Israel also, as we see from 2 Samuel 5:3. But as we see from 2 Samuel 2:7, it was really God Who was behind all such anointing of one to a position of leadership as king over the nation of Israel.

And so, during The Lord Jesus Christ's first coming from Heaven to earth, He came as King over the nation of Israel, being born into this world as such, noting Jeremiah 23:5; Matthew 2:1,2; and Zechariah 9:9 with Matthew 21:1-11. However God's Son was rejected by the leadership, as representing the nation of Israel, at His first coming from Heaven to earth, noting John 19:12-15. What this means then is that The Son's acceptance as King by the nation of Israel awaits its fulfillment as we see at Daniel 9:24, when it will be time "to anoint the most holy," which is a reference to when God's Son, The Lord Jesus Christ, as The Most Holy, is anointed King at the second stage of His second coming from Heaven to earth at the end of the last week, or seven years remaining of the 70th week, or 490 years, of the second age of time. God's Son has already been anointed High Priest and Prophet at His first coming from Heaven to earth, leaving only His being anointed as King, which anointing is in view here when He is anointed by the nation Israel as King, which will not be until the end of that 70th week, which is yet to come.

If we likewise now go on to look at Daniel 9:25 in greater detail, we see that Daniel was told, "So you are to know and discern that from the issuing of a decree (literally 'word') to restore and rebuild Jerusalem until Messiah the Prince there will be seven weeks and sixty-two weeks; it will be built again, with plaza and moat, even in times of distress." Therefore, we are to see here that from the month of Nissan of Artaxerxes twentieth year – since we have seen this is when and by whom the "decree to restore and rebuild Jerusalem" was given – "until Messiah the Prince," which we have also seen is a reference to God's Son, The Lord Jesus Christ, and specifically to the moment of His death at the cross; "there will be seven weeks and sixty-two weeks," that is, 69 weeks or 483 years!

And before we go on to look at the remainder of the sentence, one question we can ask here is: Why did God not simply say '69 weeks?' In other words, why break up the 69 weeks into 7 weeks and 62 weeks? And since we know that God always has a reason for all that He does, then we know that there must be a reason here also. So the question also becomes: What took place 7 weeks, or 49 years, after the issuing of the decree, which would seem to be what God wants us to notice here?

We have already seen earlier that working backwards 483 years from 33 AD brings us to 449 BC. If we take 7 weeks or 49 years from that we are at 400 BC. Then what is interesting to note is that God is then silent for approximately the next 400 years, until He starts to give the revelation relating to what is found in the New Testament, which is when we see the time for the fulfillment of all prophecy given under the Old Testament having now arrived, specifically with the arrival on the world scene from Heaven to earth of God's precious Son, The Lord Jesus Christ!

So we should not be surprised to hear God say at Matthew 1:1, after being silent for approximately 400 years, "The record of the genealogy of Jesus the Messiah (which word means 'Anointed One'), the son of David, the son of Abraham." And then we see that the 62 weeks or 434 years takes us from 400 BC to 33 AD. Therefore, it appears that what God wanted to make us aware of is the cutoff point for when He would stop the revelation given to mankind under the Old Testament, which is at 400 BC!

Then we note that in the rest of verse 9:25 God goes on to disclose to Daniel that "it will be built again, with plaza and moat, even in times of distress." Since the city of Jerusalem was in view before this statement, it is reasonable to now view the word "it" as referring to the city of Jerusalem. And what would also be helpful here is determining what the words "built again" and "plaza and moat" mean.

To begin with, the word "built," speaks of constructing, and when seen with the word "again," then we know that it is in reference to something which had once been destroyed. Then we further note the word "plaza" refers to open places or squares, while the word "moat" is an apparent reference to a trench, while the word "times" is in reference to the period of time in which the rebuilding takes place; with the word "distress" then referring to a time of constraint. We should also note here that in the Hebrew, the statement literally reads, 'return and be builded, wall, or, breach, or, ditch, even straight of times.'

This then relates to when both the city of Jerusalem and the temple were destroyed, which was in 486 BC; with both being then subsequently rebuilt, first the temple, as we see at Ezra 6:15, and then the city of Jerusalem being later rebuilt during the time of Nehemiah, which was indeed with difficulty; with the decree to start the rebuilding of the city having been given by Artaxerxes in the 20th year of his reign, as we have seen from Nehemiah 2:1.

And this brings up a question here, which is whether the rebuilding of the city of Jerusalem is in reference to the time of Nehemiah, or if this refers to a time yet future? In now seeking some answers, we are to note that the only time that God mentions the rebuilding the city of Jerusalem itself is in the time of Nehemiah, as we have seen. Therefore, we would conclude at this time that the statement at Daniel 9:25, "it will be built again, with plaza and moat, even in times of distress," appears to be a reference to the city of Jerusalem being rebuilt at the time of Nehemiah, as we see from Nehemiah 2:1 onwards. If one reads this portion of God's word, it is clear that the city of Jerusalem was indeed rebuilt at that time and it was "in times of distress."

Then what would also be helpful here is noting from Daniel 9:1 that what was taking place here was, "In the first year of Darius the son of Ahasuerus, of Median descent, who was made king over the kingdom of the Chaldeans," which we know was when the kingdom of Babylon was turned over to the Medes and Persians, in accordance with Daniel 5:28,31, which was at 516 BC. And above, we have also determined that the issuing of the decree by Artaxerxes, which enabled Nehemiah to lead in the rebuilding of Jerusalem, was not issued until 449 BC, which was about 77 years after Daniel was told this by God, which indeed makes it in the future. Therefore, we will conclude here again at this time that the city of Jerusalem is indeed in view at Daniel 9:25, in the words "it will be built again," with that rebuilding being what is in view at Nehemiah 2:1 and following.

If we then continue to look in detail at Daniel 9:26, of what takes place during those 70 weeks, or 490 years, Daniel was then told, "Then after the sixty-two weeks the Messiah will be cut off and have nothing, and the people of the prince who is to come will destroy the city and the sanctuary." We have already noted that the end point for 62 weeks, which is 434 years, is the death of God's precious Son, The Lord Jesus Christ, at the cross, which is what the words "the Messiah will be cut off" mean here. When we are then told that He will "have nothing," we are to realize that the words "have nothing" are one word in the Hebrew, with this word always being used negatively and always determined by the context.

And so, to help us understand what the "have nothing" would be in reference to here, let us note what the message was to the nation of Israel, first by John the Baptist, and then by God's Son Himself, after John had been imprisoned, which message we read at Matthew 4:17, "From that time Jesus began to preach and say, "Repent, for the kingdom of heaven is at hand." " It is clear from the context in Matthew that God's Son was saying this to the leadership, as representing the nation of Israel. And if they had repented, then "the kingdom of heaven" would have been established on earth, with God's Son as King.

However, we know what the outcome was, which God has had recorded for us beginning at Matthew 21:4,5, where we are told, "[4] This took place to fulfill what was spoken through the prophet (at Zechariah 9:9): [5] "Say to the daughter of Zion (in reference to the city of Jerusalem, as the capital of the nation of Israel, where the leadership was ruling from), 'Behold your King is coming to you, gentle, and mounted on a donkey, even on a colt, the foal of a beast of burden;' " as what was true from God's perspective. Then let us note the interchange between the Roman governor, Pilate, and the leadership of the nation of Israel in unbelief, relating to accepting God's Son as King, at Mark 15:9-13, "[9] Pilate answered them, saying, "Do you want me to release for you the King of the Jews?" [10] For he was aware that the chief priests had handed Him over because of envy. [11] But the chief priests stirred up the crowd to ask him to release Barabbas for them instead. [12] Answering again, Pilate said to them, "Then what shall I do with Him whom you call the King of the Jews?" [13] They shouted back, "Crucify Him!" "

And so that is exactly what happened, they crucified Him, so that God's Son, The Lord Jesus Christ, was "cut off" and "have nothing," in terms of being rejected as King by the leadership, on behalf of the nation of Israel yet in unbelief, so that the Kingdom of Heaven could not be established at that time, as what is referred to as "have nothing." What this means then is that it will be as we have already noted earlier, in that God's Son, The Lord Jesus Christ, will not be anointed as King by the nation of Israel, and His Kingdom, which is the Kingdom of Heaven, will not be established on earth, until He returns from Heaven to earth at the end of 70th week!

Then as we continue, we see that it is further revealed to Daniel at verse 9:26 that "the people of the prince who is to come will destroy the city and the sanctuary." The first thing to keep in mind here is that this is "after the sixty-two weeks," which means after God's Son had been crucified, which event was still during the second age of time. What we then need to do is identify this "prince who is to come," in order to then be able to identify "the people of the prince." The word "prince" here refers to a ruler, that is, a leader. This is the same word which was used by God when speaking of His Son at Daniel 9:25, when referring to Him as "Messiah The Prince."

And what is also very important to understand regarding this word "prince" is that what is in view here is a king in waiting. And we know this to be the case for sure due to having seen at Daniel 9:25 that God's Son, The Lord Jesus Christ, was called, "Messiah The Prince," Who is indeed a King in waiting. And so, the import of this here at verse 9:26, when speaking of "the prince who is to come," is that now we have the devil's counterfeit to "Messiah The Prince," in the one who is here "the prince who is to come," that being a character whom God later reveals at 1 John 2:18 by the term "antichrist." Since God's Son is a King in waiting, so he too, the antichrist, is a king in waiting, as the "prince who is to come" here.

And since the antichrist is in view here, who only comes to rule over the nations of the earth at the beginning of the seventh week left of the 70 week prophecy, as is clear from Revelation 13:1-8, then we know that his coming is an event which only takes place AFTER the present third age of time. Since it was the Roman empire which was ruling on earth at the time the 69th week ended with the death of God's Son, The Lord Jesus Christ, which was when the second age was interrupted to bring in the present third age; then we know that when the second age resumes again, to complete it with the last week left of the prophecy, which will be after the present third age, then it will still be the remnant of the Roman empire that will be ruling the earth, which we can term 'a revived Roman empire; and let us also keep in mind that it is the countries of present day Europe which makes up that revived Roman empire!

What this means then is that the Romans are therefore in view here as "the people of the prince who is to come," but spoken of in a time past and not in the last week of the prophecy, since we are told that the antichrist, as the prince, is yet to come, which is only in the last week. What this further means here then is that when we are told that "the people of the prince who is to come will destroy the city and the sanctuary," we are to realize that the only event this could refer to is the destruction of the city of Jerusalem and the temple, which took place at the hands of the Romans in 70 AD. And what would have been destroyed at that time is that second temple we have seen being rebuilt in the book of Ezra, and the city of Jerusalem that we saw go up again in the book of Nehemiah!

And since the city of Jerusalem and the temple were destroyed by the Romans in 70 AD, then this would mean that both need to be rebuilt again before the last week of the 70 week prophecy. Since we do see the temple being rebuilt again at Ezekiel 40:1 to Ezekiel 43:12, then this would mean that the city of Jerusalem is also seen as rebuilt before the last week of the prophecy of the 70 week, which therefore means that there was a future aspect also to the earlier statement of Daniel 9:25, "it will be built again, with plaza and moat, even in times of distress." In other words, that did not just mean to the rebuilding of the city of Jerusalem at the time of Nehemiah!

Then we further note what Daniel is told in the remainder of verse 9:26, "And its end *will come* with a flood; even to the end there will be war; desolations are determined." We are to realize that here God is giving us a summarizing account of what takes place during that seven year period, which is the 70th week of the prophecy of Daniel 9:24-27. We would benefit in looking at the same statement here in the American Standard Bible, where we read the following, "and the end thereof shall be with a flood, and even unto the end shall be war; desolations are determined."

And what would also be helpful is to know the meaning of "its end," in terms of what is here in view. The word "end," which appears twice is used in the context of a time of judgment in both instances; with the word "flood" also being used in the context of judgment. And so, what we have in view here is that the last remaining week of seven years of the 70 week, or 490 year prophecy, deals with God's judgments, which come in like a flood during that week, growing in intensity as time progresses. That this is so is clear from Revelation 6:1 to Revelation 19:21, where God gives us a picture of that seventh last week of the prophecy and where we see that this portion of God's word does indeed show God's judgments increasing in intensity as this final week of seven years runs its course!

For instance, when we read at Daniel 9:26, "even to the end there will be war; desolations are determined," we are to note that Revelation 6 begins with the antichrist coming on the world scene at the beginning of the seventh week and making war, noting for instance what we read at Revelation 6:2, "I looked, and behold, a white horse, and he who sat on it had a bow; and a crown was given to him, and he went out conquering and to conquer," and then as that seventh week ends, we see The Son of God coming from Heaven to make war against the antichrist and the false prophet, as we see at Revelation 19:11,20, Whose coming puts an end to these two evil characters, "[11] And I saw heaven opened, and behold, a white horse, and He who sat on it is called Faithful and True, and in righteousness He judges and wages war... [20] And the beast (who is the antichrist) was seized, and with him the false prophet who performed the signs in his presence, by which he deceived those who had received the mark of the beast and those who worshiped his image; these two were thrown alive into the lake of fire which burns with brimstone."

And so we see the truth of Daniel 9:26 here in the book of Revelation in that "even to the end there will be war; desolations are determined." We must realize here that the word "war" is not just speaking of battles between nations of earth, but also of a battle at the end of the seventieth week between the nations in unbelief and God; while the word "desolations" is the result of the wars on earth just mentioned; with the word "determined" meaning here that these things have been decreed by God and therefore will happen as God has said in His word!

And now, with the last week of the prophecy having been introduced in the last part of Daniel 9:26, God goes on to disclose to Daniel at verse 9:27, as relating to what the antichrist will do in the seventieth week, namely that " And he will make a firm covenant with the many for one week," with the "he" in view here being "the prince who is to come" of verse 9:26, whom we have seen is a reference to the antichrist. And so at the beginning of his rule, the antichrist "will make a firm covenant with the many for one week."

And since there is only one week of seven years left of the prophecy, and the antichrist makes a firm covenant for one week, then this means that this firm covenant here MUST BE at the beginning of his rule. And it is the antichrist who is said to make this covenant "with the many," indicating more than one nation here. And what is very important for us to realize and keep in mind is that the antichrist will be the political leader of a one world government during the last seven years left of the second age of time, while the false prophet, who comes on the scene only in the last three and a half years of that seven years, will be the leader of the false religious system on earth, which Cain instituted as the first human being to live and die in unbelief at the beginning of the first age of time.

And what is also very important for us to be aware of is that the antichrist and false prophet to come will not only be tools of the devil and under his power during that seven years to come, but that both will actually be demons in male human form, as what all angelic beings take on when entering our physical realm from the spiritual realm. This is a truth which was discovered when writing my fourth book, titled, "Have You Ever Wondered What Happens After Death," and which was subsequently confirmed when writing my twelfth book, titled, "The Mysterious World Of Angels and Demons."

And so, we are to view the making of this covenant or treaty at Daniel 9:27 as more like a document dictated by the one, that being the antichrist, who is not only in a position of superior strength, but also at the height of arrogance and deception, which the other nations of mere men would have to abide by. Then what is also important to see here is that this "firm covenant" no doubt relates to the nation of Israel itself, with our knowing this based on what we next read at Daniel 9:27, "but in the middle of the week he will put a stop to sacrifice and grain offering," with the mention of "sacrifice and grain offering" no doubt having reference to activity taking place at the rebuilt third temple in Jerusalem, which God gave the plan for at Ezekiel 40:1 to 43:12, as earlier mentioned.

And let us also remember that the last week itself pertains specifically to the nation of Israel, recalling from Daniel 9:24 that "seventy weeks have been decreed for your people and your holy city," which had reference to the nation of Israel and its capital, Jerusalem. And of course the reason that we have animal sacrifices and offerings again is because this is the last week of the second age of time, when God is again dealing with the nations of the earth through the believing remnant of the nation of Israel, so that in God's sight it is just as if the present third age of time had not taken place, since the nation of Israel has rejected God's precious Son, The Lord Jesus Christ, which was at the cut off point of the 69th week, which was still in the second age of time.

And when we read that it will be "in the middle of the week" that "he," the antichrist, "will put a stop to sacrifice and grain offering," then we are to be aware that since the week is seven years, then the mid-point of the week must be after three and a half years has elapsed of the seven years. The event which we have in view here at the hands of the antichrist, in terms of putting "a stop to sacrifice and grain offering," is in view at Matthew 24:15 and Mark 13:14.

And so we see that at the three and a half year point there is a transition taking place, from a sacrificial system that God originally ordained and is being carried out by the nation of Israel on behalf of all nations, to a system of worship which is Satanic in nature and totally anti-God. We must also remember that what the devil has been attempting to do from the beginning of creation is to replace God as being over creation, so that he counterfeits everything God does by offering man a substitute for what God provides. At Matthew 4:8-10, we even see the devil ask God's Son, The Lord Jesus Christ, to bow down and give him worship! So we know that this is what the devil is looking for, to have a kingdom where he is king, with subjects that will be willingly serving him. That is why the devil is counterfeit to The Father, while the antichrist is the counterfeit to God's Son, and the false prophet is the counterfeit to The Holy Spirit in the devil's scheme of things, simply because he is intent on setting up a counterfeit kingdom to that of God!

God only allows this to take place to show the full extent of evil during the four ages of time, before God brings evil to a complete end as time itself ends and eternity begins. We have noted from Revelation 19:20 that God does away with the antichrist and the false prophet in the lake of fire forever, which is at the return again of God's Son from Heaven to earth at the end of the last seven years left of the second age of time. But that did not include the devil. However, we do see from Revelation 20:1-3 that the devil is placed in the abyss below this present earth for the duration of the fourth age of time, which will be for a 1000 years. Then at the end of the fourth age, after those 1000 years, the devil will be released from his prison, as we see from Revelation 20:7-10, in order to lead the unbelievers of earth into one last battle against God, after which the devil will then be cast into the lake of fire, to remain there forever and ever!

Then we note that God closes the prophecy to Daniel at verse 9:27 with the words, "and on the wing of abominations *will come* one who makes desolate, even until a complete destruction, one that is decreed, is poured out on the one who makes desolate." What is critical to see here is that when we read here, "on the wing of abominations *will come* one who makes desolate...," we are to realize that this is in reference to God's own precious Son, The

Lord Jesus Christ, Who comes again to earth from Heaven at the end of the seventh week, which is here in view, to establish God's Kingdom of Heaven over the earth, with Himself as anointed King.

And when we further read in the last part of the sentence, "is poured out on the one who makes desolate," we now need to realize that the antichrist is here in view, as the one whom God's Son will now deal with at His coming, as is clear from what we see from Revelation 19:11-20. And this is precisely what we see taking place here in this last statement at Daniel 9:27, in that God intervenes in what the devil is attempting to do on earth, in terms of establishing his own kingdom through the antichrist and the false prophet, as a counterfeit to God's own Kingdom, that His Son is about to come to earth to establish and rule over during the fourth age of time.

If we look at the meaning of the words involved here, we note that the word "wing" finds its meaning in the word which follows, which is "abominations," in reference to what is detestable in God's sight, which would be the idolatrous worship now under the false prophet, exercising authority under the antichrist during the last three and a half years of the seventh week left of the prophecy. This has already been alluded to earlier, as what we see occurring from Revelation 13:11-18.

We know that not just the setting up of an abomination on the altar at the temple is in view here, since the word "abominations" is plural, which means that all the idolatrous system of worship which follows is detestable to God, which culminates in the coming of God's Son to earth again to put a stop to it, by first dealing with the antichrist and the false prophet, as we have seen at Revelation 19:20. And so we see here that on the heels of this idol worship on earth comes One Who "makes desolate... the one who makes desolate," with the words "makes desolate" being one word in the Hebrew, that being "Shamem," meaning to bring devastation to the physical landscape and wretchedness to human beings. For believers of earth, this last seven years is a horrid time of tribulation at the hands of the antichrist and the false prophet; but for all unbelievers, it will be an even more terrible time under the direct judgment of God!

Then the words a "complete destruction" is also one word in the original Hebrew, that being "Kala," meaning 'a full end,' which is "one that is decreed," with the word "decreed" being "Haras" in the original, as what has been determined and cannot be changed or altered. The words "poured out" is also one word in the Hebrew, being "Natak." And so we see that on the heels of all the abominations of the false prophet under the antichrist in the last three and a half years of their rule, The Son of God will come and bring to an end the antichrist, the false prophet, and all unbelievers of earth, pouring upon them the full wrath of God, which has been determined.

As we close this prophecy of Daniel 9:24-27, namely the 70 weeks of 490 years, there are two truths to note here. The first is that the 70 weeks of 490 years parallels the period of time which God calls, "the times of the Gentiles" at Luke 21:24, where we read, "and they will fall by the edge of the sword, and will be led captive into all the nations; and Jerusalem will be trampled under foot by the Gentiles UNTIL THE TIMES OF THE GENTILES ARE FULFILLED." In other words, this is the time period from the exile to Babylon of the nation of Israel (that being from the third deportation of 586 BC, when the temple and the city of Jerusalem were destroyed), which means Israel was from that point on is under Gentile domination in the world, until the coming to earth again of God's Son, The Lord Jesus Christ, at the end of the last seven years, that is, at the end of Daniels' 70th week of Daniel 9:24-27, to now establish God's Kingdom of Heaven and to rule over the nations of the earth during the fourth age of time, which will be for a thousand years.

Then the second truth for us to keep in mind from Daniel 9:24-27 is that "from the issuing of a decree to restore and rebuild Jerusalem until Messiah the Prince there will be seven weeks and sixty-two weeks..." In other words, by the time God's Son comes to provide atonement for mankind, through His death at the cross, God says there will be 69 weeks of the 70 weeks will have gone by, which means one week will be left to run its course of that second age of time, WITH THE PRESENT THIRD AGE RUNNING ITS COURSE BEFORE THAT LAST WEEK TAKES PLACE! Since we are still in the third age of time, then that means that last week, including the coming of the antichrist, is yet future to us alive at the moment, awaiting the time when God completes the present third age of time, which by all current indications could be any day!

"He made known to us the mystery of His will, according to His kind intention which He purposed in Him…"

Ephesians 1:9

CHAPTER FOUR

/ Seeing from God's word that the present third age of time was never seen during the second age of time, and so, when God resumes the second age in order to complete the last seven years of it, there will be no knowledge of this present third age!

FIRST then, because the second age of time – which goes from Genesis 12:1 to the end of Acts 1 in God's word – was interrupted at the death of God's Son, with its seven remaining years being completed only after the present third age of time ends, means that God never allowed those who lived during the first and second ages of time to see the present third age of time in prophecy, which truth God only revealed to believers of the present third age after it had started at Acts 2!

So let us read what God says at Ephesians 3:4-11, to begin with, where He makes this clear, adding capitalization and notes in brackets as a help, "[4] By referring to this, when you read you can understand my insight into the mystery of Christ, [5] WHICH IN OTHER GENERATIONS (that is, relating to the ages before the present third age, that being the first and second ages of time) WAS NOT MADE KNOWN TO THE SONS OF MEN, AS IT HAS NOW BEEN REVEALED TO HIS HOLY APOSTLES AND PROPHETS (of the present third age) IN THE SPIRIT; [6] to be specific, that the Gentiles are fellow heirs and fellow members of the body, and fellow partakers of the promise in Christ Jesus through the gospel, [7] of which I was made a minister, according to the gift of God's grace which was given to me according to the working of His power. [8] To me, the very least of all saints, this grace was given, to preach to the Gentiles the unfathomable riches of Christ, [9] AND TO BRING TO LIGHT WHAT IS THE ADMINISTRATION OF THE MYSTERY WHICH FOR AGES (that is, the first and second ages of time) HAS BEEN HIDDEN IN GOD who created all things; [10] SO THAT THE MANIFOLD WISDOM OF GOD MIGHT NOW BE MADE KNOWN THROUGH THE CHURCH (during the third age of time) to the rulers and the authorities in the heavenly places. [11] THIS WAS IN ACCORDANCE WITH THE ETERNAL PURPOSE which He carried out in Christ Jesus our Lord…"

And now let us also notice what God says at Colossians 1:25-27 relating to the same truth, "[25] Of this church I was made a minister according to the stewardship from God bestowed on me for your benefit, so that I might fully carry out the preaching of the word of God, [26] that is, THE MYSTERY WHICH HAS BEEN HIDDEN FROM THE PAST AGES (that is, the first and second ages of time) AND GENERATIONS, BUT HAS NOW (in the present third age of time) BEEN MANIFESTED TO HIS SAINTS (that is, to believers), [27] TO WHOM GOD WILLED TO MAKE KNOWN WHAT IS THE RICHES OF THE GLORY OF THIS MYSTERY among the Gentiles, WHICH IS CHRIST IN YOU, THE HOPE OF GLORY."

What this means then is that all the spiritual truth that God revealed in His word, that is, from Acts 2 to Revelation 5, is a truth that was hidden from believers during the first two ages of time, which takes in God's word from Genesis 1:1 to the end of Acts 1. And this truth now leads to the second truth that we want to bring to light in this chapter.

The SECOND truth then is that whenever the present third age of time ends and God resumes the second age of time in order to complete the last seven years left of that age, which further means that during this seven years remaining of the second age of time God returns to ruling over the people of the earth through the believers of the nation of Israel, as it was before the second age was interrupted in 33 AD with the death of God's Son at the cross. And not only that, but we are also to see that as God resumes the last seven years of the second age of time, IT WILL BE AS IF THE PRESENT THIRD AGE OF TIME HAD NEVER OCCURRED!

What this means then is that as God resumes the second age to complete it with the seven years remaining of it, after this present third age ends, then there will be NO KNOWLEDGE OR REMEMBRANCE WHATSOEVER OF THIS PRESENT THIRD AGE! This is why, for instance, that we see at Ezekiel 40 to 48, which has to do solely with the last seven years left of the second age of time, that we see THE THIRD TEMPLE being rebuilt in Jerusalem in Israel, WITH ANIMAL SACRIFICES AND OFFERINGS RESUMING AGAIN, since that is how things were before this present third age started, and this is what needs to be reverted to as the second age resumes again! This is very important to grasp and be aware of as one reads and studies God's word!

Those animal sacrifices and offerings during the first two ages of time were but foreshadowing the work which God's Son would one day do, once He came to earth as born of a woman, as God prophesied at Genesis 3:15. And since that whole system of religion that God instituted for the nation of Israel through Moses was now being reverted to in the last seven years left of the second age of time meant, as we have indicated in this chapter, that the present third age of time was never prophesied before it started with the coming of The Holy Spirit at Acts 2:1, and also meant that mankind will have no knowledge of the truth God has made known relating to Acts 2:1 to the end of Revelation 5 once the second age resumes again to complete it, after the present third age has ended!

When Russia went into Ukraine on February 24, 2022, it immediately divided the nations of the world into those who opposed Russia's move and those who supported Russia's move. The Biblical import of this is that we now have the alignment of nations that was required to have the antichrist enter the world scene, as God describes at Revelation 6!

CHAPTER FIVE

/ The present day alignment of the nations of the earth is exactly in line with the military conflicts we see occurring at Revelation 6, which is when the antichrist makes his entry on the world scene!

When Russia went into Ukraine on February 24, 2022, it immediately divided the nations of the world into those who opposed Russia's move and those who supported Russia's move. The Biblical import of this is that we now have the alignment of nations that was required to have the antichrist enter the world scene, as God describes at Revelation Chapter 6!

But before we look at Revelation Chapter 6, we first need to have a little background information regarding the book of Revelation, for any who might not be that familiar with that book of God's word. There are 22 Chapters in the book of Revelation. And we are to note that God makes a very important statement at Revelation 1:19, where we read, "Therefore write the things which you have seen, and the things which are, and the things which will take place after these things," here indicating that what the apostle John was writing down as the book of Revelation could be divided into three parts, namely: 1) "the things which you have seen," in reference to Revelation 1, and especially the vision of God's Son in glory, which John sees at verses 1:12-16; 2) "the things which are," in reference to Revelation 2 and 3, specifically relating to the course of the present third age of time, which the seven literal local churches are being used by God to give us a picture of in outline form; and 3) "the things which will take place after these things," now in reference to Revelation 4:1 to 22:5.

What we then need to note is that this third section, namely Revelation 4 to the end of Revelation 22, can be further divided into three parts, with Revelation 4 and 5 being intended by God to be a picture of God's church in Heaven, which is all the believers of earth of the present third age of time being there at that time in glorified bodies, while the events of the last seven years of the second age of time are taking place on earth, which is then the second event in this third section, beginning at Revelation 6! In other words, Revelation 4 and 5 is what takes place in Heaven while Revelation 6:1 to 19:21 takes place on earth during the exact same seven year period! Then in the last part of section three, we have the fourth age of time, where we see God bring to a consummation in time through His Son, The Lord Jesus Christ, all He began to do at the time of the original creation at Genesis 1:1!

And so, the part of Revelation that will concern us in this chapter is Revelation 6 to Revelation 19:21, which are events that take place on earth during the last seven years left of the second age of time, which begins with the entry of the devil's antichrist on the world scene! However, there is one further word of background information that is needed here before we begin to discuss this event, which is that God has divided that seven year period into two sections. In the first section, which goes from Revelation 6:1 to Revelation 11:19, God has the apostle John in Heaven describing events which he sees, which goes from the entry of the antichrist on the world scene at Revelation 6:1 and takes us to the end of time. Then at Revelation 12:1 to the end of Revelation 22, God has the apostle John look at the same time period again, but now focusing on only certain events and with far greater detail!

And so, in having this as background, let us now note what God tells us at Revelation 6:1-8 for our present purpose, of what will happen when the antichrist makes his entry on the world scene, which as we will now see could occur at any moment, because nations are now aligned for this to occur! And so, let us note Revelation 6:1,2 to begin with here, *"[1] Then I saw when the Lamb broke one of the seven seals, and I heard one of the four living creatures saying as with a voice of thunder, "Come." [2] I looked, and behold, a white horse, and he who sat on it had a bow; and a crown* was given to him, and he went out conquering and to conquer."

When we read here, "Then I saw...," we are to keep in mind that this is the apostle John as still in Heaven, being allowed of God to see what takes place on earth. So the first thing that John saw was, "the Lamb broke one of the seven seals," this would be the first seal of the seven seals of the book, which God's Son had taken from His Father's Hand, as we see at Revelation 5:7.

And as that first seal is broken, we are further told what John next saw and heard in Heaven, "and I heard one of the four living creatures saying as with a voice of thunder, "Come." So we see here that the living creatures are involved in more than just giving God worship, in that they are also involved in carrying out God's commands, same as with God's other orders of angelic beings (noting Psalm 103:20). We are not told which one of the four living creatures was first called forth by God to carry out a command here, only that it was "one of the four living creatures..."

Then we are to see that this was said by this living creature, "as with a voice of thunder," for the simple reason that this is being said all the way from Heaven to earth, to one who is not a believer and is actually opposed to God, that being the antichrist, as we will see next. And since God is in control of all that exists, being Sovereign and God Almighty, then He has authority over even opposing forces led by Satan, the devil, and all the fallen angels with him. This means that the word "Come" is now God's signal to indicate that He is permitting the forces of evil to work on earth under the devil's direction.

Then as a result of the first living creature having said, "Come," the apostle John, from Heaven, now looks and sees on earth A WHITE HORSE, with its rider being seen as having two things here. The one being a BOW and the other a CROWN, with the significance of both being revealed to us here, which is that, "he went out conquering and to conquer." The fact that it is a "he" on the white horse indicates that it is a male figure.

And what also needs to be grasped here is that this scene is on earth and not in Heaven, for the male figure on the white horse is the ANTICHRIST, which is why he is shown riding on a white horse, because in the design of the devil, the antichrist not only OPPOSES God's Son, The Lord Jesus Christ, but seeks to COUNTERFEIT Him, for when God's Son is later seen coming to earth at Revelation 19:11, at the end of seven years of the second age of time there in view, it is as riding on a while horse!

That it is the antichrist who is in view here at Revelation 6:2, riding a white horse, is due to this being a fulfillment of God's prophecy at Daniel 9:24-27, which would be beneficial for us to note here again for our present purpose, "[24] Seventy weeks have been decreed for your people and your holy city, to finish the transgression, to make an end of sin, to make atonement for iniquity, to bring in everlasting righteousness, to seal up vision and prophecy and to anoint the most holy place. [25] So you are to know and discern that from the issuing of a decree to restore and rebuild Jerusalem until Messiah the Prince there will be seven weeks and sixty-two weeks; it will be built again, with plaza and moat, even in times of distress. [26] Then after the sixty-two weeks the Messiah will be cut off and have nothing, and the people of the prince who is to come will destroy the city and the sanctuary. And its end will come with a flood; even to the end there will be war; desolations are determined. [27] And he will make a firm covenant with the many for one week, but in the middle of the week he will put a stop to sacrifice and grain offering; and on the wing of abominations will come one who makes desolate, even until a complete destruction, one that is decreed, is poured out on the one who makes desolate."

We see from verse 9:24 here that 70 weeks, or 490 years, have been decreed relating to the nation of Israel and the city of Jerusalem, its capital. This 490 years needs to be seen as also being the time period known as, "the times of the Gentiles," that God mentions at Luke 21:24, "and they (the people of the nation of Israel) will fall by the edge of the sword, and will be led captive into all the nations (referring to their exile to Babylon in 486 BC); and Jerusalem will be trampled under foot by the Gentiles until the times of the Gentiles are fulfilled," and where we see that Jerusalem will be under Gentile control for that period of time.

Then at Daniel 9:25 above, we see that there are 62 weeks and 7 weeks from the issuing of the decree, which is when the 490 years begins to be counted, until "Messiah The Prince," which is a reference to God's Son, at His first coming from Heaven to earth, with 69 weeks, which is 483 years, having expired to the very day by the time Messiah is cut off, that is, dies for a sinful human race on the cross. What this means then is that there is one week , or seven years, remaining of the decreed 70 weeks for Gentile domination of Jerusalem.

And this is where we now see the final week begin here at Revelation 6, with the coming of the antichrist, who is in view at Daniel 9:27 where we read, "And he will make a firm covenant with the many for one week (seven years), but in the middle of the week (that is, at the three and half year mark) he will put a stop to sacrifice and grain offering..." From the context and from a study of the book of Daniel in detail, we know that the "he" in view here is the antichrist and that the "one week" in view here is not only the 70th week of God's prophecy through the prophet Daniel, but is also the last week of seven years remaining of the second age of time, when God will again be dealing with the nations of the earth through the believers of the nation of Israel, and not through the believers making up God's church on earth, as is the case during the present third age of time. And so, this is indeed the antichrist here in view at Revelation 6:2 and this is indeed during a time of God's judgment against all the unbelievers of earth!

And before we go further, we should make a few comments regarding some of the words encountered here at Revelation 6:2, namely the word "bow," which is "Toxon." The word "bow" was used for two purposes in God's word, namely to hunt, as at Genesis 27:3, and also to do battle, as for instance at 1 Kings 22:34. Here at Revelation 6:2, it is to be seen as being for battle. Then the word "crown," which is "Stephanos," as that which encircles or surrounds the head, which here denotes a victor's crown, as one beginning his rule, which is made clear from the description which follows in the words "conquering" and "to conquer." And so, the word "conquering," and the word "conquer," are both "Nikao" in the original Greek, meaning 'to carry off the victory,' or 'to come off victorious.' So when we read that the antichrist is seen as "conquering," that is when he is attacked by other forces and carries off the victory; while when we see him go out "to conquer," that is when he is the one attacking others and comes off victorious. In either case, the antichrist is seen as being victorious over all earthly enemies here!

And before we speak of the worldwide war that would be taking place on earth at this time, and the nations that would be involved, in terms of those aligned with one another, and those in the opposing camp, let us first look at what God tells us next at Revelation 6:3,4, *"[3] When He* (God's Son) *broke the second seal, I heard the second living creature saying, "Come." [4] And another, a red horse, went out; and to him who sat on it, it was granted to take peace from the earth, and that men would slay one another; and a great sword was given to him."*

And as a result of the second living creature saying, "Come," we see "another," in reference to another horse now going forth on the earth, this time "a red horse..." Again, we see a male figure riding this red horse, and to him, "it was granted to take peace from the earth... and a great sword was given to him." And as a result of his having taken peace from the earth, we see that this was so, "that men would slay one another..." In other words, this means that the unbelievers among mankind, who are the ones left on earth, are now at war with one another!

The first rider on the white horse has been identified as the antichrist, so the obvious question now becomes, "who is the rider on the red horse"? And in order to answer this question, we need to realize that in order for the antichrist to be conquering and going out to conquer, THERE NEEDS TO BE OPPOSITION, which is what the red horse represents here. In other words, all the opposing forces of earth, who are all unbelievers, are seen fighting AGAINST THE ANTICHRIST AND HIS FORCES!

If it be asked why unbelievers would be fighting against unbelievers, the simple answer is that unbelievers have been fighting one another since the dawn of human history and is one way God deals with them in judgment! We are given a prime example of this later at Revelation 17:17, where we read of the unbelievers of earth, "For God has put it in their hearts to execute His purpose by having a common purpose, and by giving their kingdom to the beast (who is here the antichrist), until the words of God will be fulfilled." So all is being outworked in accordance with God's plan for these last seven years, which is to put to death every unbeliever (noting Hebrews 9:27), who are not elect of God, before this seven year period ends. And God's way of putting them to death is to have them fight each other!

What also needs to be remembered here is that the devil is never opposed to any unbelievers being put to death, for he knows that all such will now be part of his kingdom in hell forever! In other words, when a person dies without knowing God through faith in His Son in salvation, then one is under the devil's dominion forever and ever. So it is to the devil's advantage to have WAR, where unbelievers kill each other, with God using this desire of the devil to accomplish His own purposes, such as to bring His judgment on the unbelievers of earth!

And this is now a good place to bring in THE PRESENT ALIGNMENT OF THE NATIONS OF THE EARTH to show that what we read here at Revelation 6:1-4 could be fulfilled at any moment! We have already seen that the antichrist will arise out the revived Roman Empire, which is present day Europe, and as a result of Russia going into Ukraine on February 24, 2022, the countries of Europe have been ALIGNED AGAINST RUSSIA. And since the countries of Europe are part of the North Atlantic Treaty Organization (NATO) means that the 30 countries comprising the NATO alliance at the moment are also all against Russia, these being: Canada, Croatia, France, Germany, Greece, Hungary, Czech Republic, Denmark, Estonia, Albania, Belgium, Bulgaria, Iceland, Luxembourg, Montenegro, Netherlands, Italy, Latvia, Lithuania, North Macedonia, Norway, Poland, Slovakia, United Kingdom, Portugal, Romania, United States, Slovenia, Spain, and Turkey.

As this book is being written, Finland and Sweden were also in the process of joining the NATO alliance. NATO also has nine other global partners, which it engages with on an individual basis. These are: Afghanistan, Australia, Colombia, Iraq, Japan, The Republic of Korea, Mongolia, New Zealand, and Pakistan.

Speaking now of countries that Russia has legally binding agreements of mutual defense with, first and foremost these are members of the Collective Security Treaty Organization (CSTO), an intergovernmental alliance created in 1992 that now unites six post-Soviet states: Russia, Armenia, Belarus, Kazakhstan, Kyrgyzstan, and Tajikistan. Then there is also the powerful BRICS alliance, which is made up of Brazil, Russia, India, China, and South Africa, with more in the process of joining, such as Iran and Argentina.

As we can see from the foregoing, these are the countries that would be found fighting against one another the moment the antichrist makes his entry on the world scene, which brings a fulfillment of Revelation 6:1-4! And the key part to keep in mind here is that the antichrist and the forces aligned with him are VICTORIOUS here over all the forces aligned with Russia, which would in reality be nothing short of World War 3! What this means then is that in any subsequent battle we see take place from Revelation 6 onward is either ALL NATIONS coming against Israel, as we see for instance at Revelation 1613,14,16, with God then giving us greater detail of this battle at Revelation 19:11-21, when God's Son now returns again from Heaven to earth to fight and defeat all these forces at the end of the seven years left of the second age of time. This is also God's fulfillment of what we earlier saw at Daniel 2:44, where we read, "In the days of those kings (which God's Son is seen here as defeating, relating to the antichrist and the forces aligned with him, which are all nations of earth) the God of heaven will set up a kingdom (that of His Son over the earth to begin the fourth age of time) which will never be destroyed, and that kingdom will not be left for another people; it will crush and put an end to all these kingdoms, but it will itself endure forever."

Then we note that the apostle John is led of God to relate what he sees take place next on earth, as we now see from Revelation 6:5,6, *"[5] When He broke the third seal, I heard the third living creature saying, "Come." I looked, and behold, a black horse; and he who sat on it had a pair of scales in his hand. [6] And I heard something like a voice in the center of the four living creatures saying, "A quart of wheat for a denarius, and three quarts of barley for a denarius; and do not damage the oil and the wine.""*

Now John sees God's Son open the third seal of the book in Heaven and immediately the third living creature in Heaven, which had "a face like that of a man," was now led to also say, "Come." And as a result of that command of God from Heaven through the living creature, there now comes forth "a black horse" on the earth, with the rider again being identified as a "he," who "had a pair of scales in his hand." Since scales are for doing business, then it is best to regard the male riding the black horse here as representing the merchants of the earth.

And what is interesting to note is that John then hears, "a voice in the center of the four living creatures saying, "A quart of wheat for a denarius, and three quarts of barley for a denarius; and do not damage the oil and the wine," which we need to realize is the voice of God The Father Himself, Who is here setting the price and giving the merchants instructions, since all is always under His absolute control, doing so while at the same time continuing His judgment against all unbelievers of earth.

What also needs to be grasped here is that the mention of the "wheat," the "barley," which are grains, along with the "oil" and the "wine," were three things that God promised the nation of Israel to provide for them when He was pleased with them, noting for instance what we read at Deuteronomy 7:12,13, "[12] Then it shall come about, because you listen to these judgments and keep and do them, that the Lord your God will keep with you His covenant and His lovingkindness which He swore to your forefathers. [13] He will love you and bless you and multiply you; He will also bless the fruit of your womb and the fruit of your ground, your GRAIN and your new WINE and your OIL, the increase of your herd and the young of your flock, in the land which He swore to your forefathers to give you."

However, when God was displeased with the nation of Israel, He would withhold these three things from them, as we see for instance at Deuteronomy 28:38-40, "[38] You shall bring out much seed to the field but you will gather in little (GRAIN), for the locust will consume it. [39] You shall plant and cultivate vineyards, but you will neither drink of the WINE nor gather the grapes, for the worm will devour them. [40] You shall have olive trees throughout your territory but you will not anoint yourself with the OIL, for your olives will drop off." What this also tells us here is that we are indeed in the second age of time again, when God is dealing with the nations of the earth through the believers of the nation of Israel.

Then what also needs to be noticed is that God uses "a denarius" for the bartering of goods. The word "denarius" is "Denarion," which we are to see from Matthew 22:17-21 was a Roman coin in daily use during the time of the first coming from Heaven to earth of God's Son, The Lord Jesus Christ, and further noting from Matthew 20:2 that it was the equivalent of a man's wages for the day, which was 12 hours of labor, from 6 am to 6 pm. Therefore, in the mention of a denarius here, we are to grasp that God is resuming the second age at exactly the same place where it was interrupted in order to bring in the third age of time. And now that the third age has been completed, God resumes the second age again in order to complete it with these seven years that are left!

We also see here that God also gives us what the going price of these are on the earth during this time of judgment, where war is taking place all over the earth. So "a quart of wheat for a denarius, and three quarts of barley for a denarius," were the going price, with wheat, as usual, being more expensive than barley, which was a more common and less valuable grain, with the price here being seen high due to men not being able to plant seed and harvest during a time of conflict, with the resulting increase in the price of goods, likely leading to scarcity, with the poorest likely having to do without!

Then when talking of the oil and the wine, God instructs mankind not to damage it, with the word "damage" here being "Adikeo," which could also have been translated 'hurt, or harm,' since the olive oil and the wine in view here were everyday staples. Since there would be a scarcity of all commodities to begin with, due to war, then it becomes imperative to conserve what there was available and not seek to destroy it during this time of war!

As is therefore clear from the foregoing, the food chain on earth has been totally disrupted due to a worldwide war going on and as a result there is widespread famine taking place on earth, seeing that as usual only the rich can afford what little is available in a time of scarcity. It is therefore clear from what we see occurring at present in the world that we are seeing the signs all around us of conditions being prepared for this to occur on a worldwide scale!

In then going on with what John was allowed of God to see next, as we now read at Revelation 6:7,8, *"[7] When the Lamb broke the fourth seal, I heard the voice of the fourth living creature saying, "Come." [8] I looked, and behold, an ashen horse; and he who sat on it had the name Death; and Hades was following with him. Authority was given to them over a fourth of the earth, to kill with sword and with famine and with pestilence and by the wild beasts of the earth."*

What John now sees and hears, as God's precious Son breaks the fourth seal of the book in Heaven, with the fourth living creature, that was like a flying eagle, now also say, "Come." And again, we see that the result on earth is to have another horse appear, which was ashen in color, with the male figure riding the horse having "the name Death." We are then told that "Hades was following with him." Hades here of course is the place under the earth that the soul and spirit of unbelievers goes to after physical death and until the time of the final judgment of Revelation 20:11-15. That is why Hades was seen following Death here.

What should also be obvious to us by now is that the rider on each horse is only representative of something taking place on earth. And so the rider on the white horse is a picture of the antichrist having now been allowed of God to begin his work on earth, not that the antichrist was literally going around on a white horse. Similarly with the red horse, it represented all the forces of opposition to the antichrist on earth, and not that there was a literal person riding a red horse. The rider on a red horse simply denotes that God allowed these forces to be active as part of His plan for what takes place during these seven years. And the same is also true in regards to the rider on the black horse, representing the dark times economically that were taking place on the earth at this time due to mankind in unbelief being involved in warfare, which did affect food production, distribution, and commerce.

And now under the fourth seal's judgment on earth, we see a rider with the name Death riding an ashen horse to represent the color of death, which is now taking place all over the earth, with the soul and spirit of these unbelievers going directly to the compartment of the unbelievers in Hades under this present earth. The equivalent word for Hades in the Old Testament is 'Sheol.'

We also need to be aware that there was also a compartment for the souls of the believers of time in Hades, since the spirit of a believer is with God at bodily death, while the body is in the grave. Since the soul has a sinful nature, then it cannot enter Heaven until the time of the first resurrection relating to believers, which is when the sinful nature is removed from a believer and when each is given a spiritual body to enter God's realm, which is spiritual.

So we should not be surprised to further read here at Revelation 6:8 that, "Authority was given to them," that is, to Death and Hades, "over a fourth of the earth, to kill with sword and with famine and with pestilence and by wild beasts of the earth." What this means then is that a fourth of the unbelievers of earth are going to perish at this time, meaning under the four seals so far unsealed by God's Son in Heaven. And we are again to see that this is indeed a resumption of the second age of time, which God has here resumed, due to the mention of the four methods by which God's judgment was meted out during the second age of time, these being "with sword," "with famine," "with pestilence," and "by the wild beasts," noting what God told the nation of Israel at Ezekiel 14:21, "For thus says the Lord God, "How much more when I send My four severe judgments against Jerusalem: sword, famine, wild beasts and plague to cut off man and beast from it!""

And so, as we end this chapter, we see that the antichrist indeed does arise out of the revived Roman Empire, which was in place at the time of the death of God's Son, and will now be seen as present day Europe, when God resumes the second age of time in order to complete it, as soon as the present third age of time ends! And it should also be clear to all of us that the nations of the earth are now aligned for the war on earth that will now be occurring as the antichrist makes his entry on the world scene, as political leader over a one world government, with all the unfortunate drastic chaos and consequences that will occur to all human beings left on earth due to that war now taking place!

CHAPTER SIX

/ Ten things the devil needs to have in place in order to bring his evil agenda to pass on earth!

In this chapter, we will be looking at ten things the devil needs to have in place, at the very least, in order to bring his agenda to pass on earth. We will only be mentioning this in brief here, as most readers will readily grasp what is being said and will be aware of this actually taking place in the countries in which each one lives. What is to be grasped here is that these ten things will be found as being more advanced in existing authoritarian regimes, such as in Communist-controlled China, for the simple reason that these countries are not only ungodly to start with, in terms of suppressing believers and the Bible, but also because they already have a form of government in place that will mirror the one world government of the antichrist when it is established on the world scene! And now, for those ten things:

1) A one world government under a one world political leader

What should be grasped here is that when the devil's antichrist is revealed upon the earth, there will ALREADY BE an established structure for a one world government to take place! We already have the United Nations (UN), with all its various agencies covering every aspect of human life on earth, as one such existing structure!

2) A one world religion under one leader

As we have seen when looking at Revelation 13:11-18, there is a religious leader coming on the world stage, as the false prophet, who will be over the false religious system of the devil. And so again, any movement on earth, such as the establishment of the World Council of Churches (WCC) in 1948 and continuing on at present, working toward unifying the religions of the world should be seen as not only moving us closer to the end of the present third age, but also leading the world toward the devil-inspired false religious systems being brought into one world religion!

3) A cashless society, which requires the introduction of a digital currency

This specifically relates to Revelation 13:17, where we saw that the antichrist, through the false prophet, will cause all those on earth who refuse to give him worship will not be able to buy or sell. And in order for that to be achieved, it is obvious that the antichrist will need to be able to control every transaction on earth, which can only be achieved if there is no cash, and all payments are digital. This also means that a digital currency and digital methods of payment must be in place, which the antichrist world government will be able to control.

4) A digital identification mark

Again, this digital identification mark (ID) is required as a means to control who buys and sells. This ID will be biometric in nature, that is, will use some part of the human body to identify that it is really you. At Revelation 13:16, God says that this ID will be either on one's right hand or on one's forehead.

5) Control of all forms of media

It is obvious that the world government under the antichrist will be in control of all forms of media, such as television, radio, internet, social media platforms, and all means of communications, so as to be able totally control what people hear, see, read, and therefore think!

6) A surveillance state

It should also be obvious that the world government that the antichrist will rule over will be able to not only identify individuals, but to also know where they are at any given moment of the day or night, including knowing what they are doing. This means that monitoring cameras, facial recognition systems, license plate readers, and drones must be in place the world over to constantly monitor people!

7) Control of population increases

It should also be obvious that the lower the population, the easier it is to control it, which further means that population increases must be minimized by whatever means may be necessary to achieve this, such as birth control methods, forced sterilization, mind control, drugs, eugenics, transhumanism, and according to Bill Gates' 2015 TED talk, even the use of vaccines!

8) A disarmed population

It should also be obvious that a world one government under the antichrist needs a disarmed population, so that people cannot defend themselves, nor rise up against the established authorities. This therefore means that all things that can be used as a weapon must be confiscated and destroyed, including their means of production!

9) Effective means of rounding up and killing off enemies of the state

The antichrist will also have at his disposal efficient means of quickly tracking down, rounding up, and eliminating any person deemed an enemy of the state. There are in existence at present killer robots, drones, and similar means, that can be programmed through artificial intelligence systems to track and kill individuals anywhere in the world.

For instance, one only needs to show a drone, that has been programmed by AI, a picture and an address of a person, and then let the drone track and kill the person with a bullet, an explosive device (if more than one at a time), or a poisonous dart. These means are all currently available!

10) Removal of the United States from being world leader; economically, militarily, and diplomatically

As everyone knows, the United States is at present (or at least was until Joe Biden) the world leader; economically, militarily, and diplomatically. The United States has been since WW1 the elephant in the room, in that it only had to speak or make a move and it affected the rest of the world. Friends and foes of the United States all knew this! That is why the devil knows that in order to bring in a one world government under the antichrist, he needs to eliminate the United States from being leader of the world, as that is a position that the world government under the antichrist must hold!

It is clear from God's word, and especially the book of Revelation, that this will indeed be the case when the antichrist does come on the world scene, in that the United States will indeed have been removed from being world leader economically, militarily, and diplomatically! And with Joe Biden's so called 'Presidency,' the United States has indeed been rendered in a very short time a third world banana republic as a gift to the evil one!

To God alone be all praise, honor, and glory, with thanksgiving, both now and forevermore! Amen, amen, and amen.

ADDENDUM A

/ The four ages of time

What is important to know when reading God's word, the Bible, is that God has divided time into four ages. And since God's word covers all of time, then all of God's word can be subdivided along the lines of these four ages. But before noting what these four ages are, we need to also be aware that in each of the four ages of time, God uses the believers of that age as His vessels. In other words, God is accomplishing His work on earth through the believers of each age of time.

And what is also important to keep in mind in regards to this is that although God starts each age with believers, before long the number of unbelievers in each age outnumbers the number of believers. In other words, one characteristic of each age of time is that there is a believing remnant among a mass of unbelievers, with these believers in each age being those whom God preserves for Himself and through whom God works to accomplish His purposes in each age through time.

And so, in the first age of time God worked through Adam and his believing descendants as His vessels to accomplish His will on earth, which age covers the first eleven chapters of Genesis. What this means is that they were the believers who willingly served Him out of love for Him. In other words, this was the believing line of descent, or the believing remnant, through which God worked out His will.

Then when we begin Genesis 12, we see God take one believer, Abraham, and out of that one man's descendants through the line of Isaac, and then through the line of Jacob, God makes a nation, which is Israel. And again, we need to see that only the believing line of descent within the nation of Israel was the remnant through which God worked to accomplish His will. What this means is that not all those who were of the nation of Israel were believers. In fact, the majority were unbelievers. Therefore, in the second age of time, which goes from Genesis 12 to the end of Malachi in the Old Testament, and includes the gospel accounts of Matthew, Mark, Luke, and John, plus Acts 1 and Revelation 6 to 19 in the New Testament, God works out His will in time through the believers of the nation of Israel, which is again a small number compared to the total number.

And here we need to pause for a moment and mention something else before going on to consider the third age of time, and this is the fact of representation. What this means is that in the first age of time, we have Adam and Eve as our first parents, who were but representative of all people on earth. In other words, God knew that what this one couple did, any other couple would have done the same thing, since God knows that once sin entered His perfect and sinless creation, we all would have the same sinful nature as human beings.

Then the same is true in regards to the nation of Israel in the second age of time, in that God knew that what this one nation did, any other nation on earth would likewise have done had it been chosen by God as a representative nation. So when God set out to make the one nation of Israel, He started out with just believers. But when the nation of Israel came into existence later, only a believing remnant within the nation were believers. Now since the nation of Israel was but representative of all the nations, then God knew that if He had chosen any other nation on earth, He would find that only a believing remnant would ever become believers to serve Him willingly out of love for Him out of a mass of unbelievers, who would now be in any of those nations. In other words, no other human being would have acted any differently than our first parents, and likewise, no other nation would have acted any differently than the nation of Israel did. This means that all human beings and all nations are likewise guilty before God!

What also needs to be mentioned here, as we now go on to look at the third age of time, is that the first two ages basically relate to the time period covered by the Old Testament, which means that the third and fourth ages of time must be covered by the New Testament portion of God's word, the Bible. And let us recall that in the first age, God worked through the believers of that age, beginning with Adam, while in the second age of time, God works through the believers of the nation of Israel, beginning with Abraham. So as we come to the third age of time, which goes from Acts 2 to the end of Revelation 5 in God's word, we have God working through all the believers of earth, whom God calls "the church."

What this means then is that in this third age of time, which we are presently still in, God is accomplishing His will through all the believers of earth, with God now not looking at any specific nation in particular. In other words, during the present third age of time, also known as 'the church age,' the nation of Israel, although being supernaturally preserved by God, is still just the same as any other nation on earth, having a believing remnant among a majority of unbelievers.

Then in the fourth age of time, which is basically covered by Revelation 20 to 22 in the New Testament, although mentioned often in prophecy in various portions of the Old Testament, we have God working through the believers of that age, but now with much greater variation. In other words, during the fourth age of time God works through the believers of every nation on earth still in their natural bodies, and also through the believers of the first three ages of time, who would have now experienced their part in the first resurrection relating to believers and who are now in their resurrected bodies! This is covered in much greater detail in my book, "An Introduction To The New World That Is Coming Upon The Earth," which focuses on this fourth age of time. If there are any readers who are not sure of what is meant by the first and second resurrection, and the fact of people serving God in their new resurrected bodies in the future, please see my book, "Have You Ever Wondered What Happens After Death?"

Before leaving this Addendum, it is also important to be aware that the Old Testament portion of God's word, the Bible, contains 39 books, which deal with the beginning of all things in God's plan of the ages, while the New Testament portion of God's word, the Bible, contains 27 books, which deal with the consummation of all things in God's eternal plan, which God is outworking through the four ages of time.

Also of great value is to know that the second age of time is not completed until AFTER the completion of the present third age of time. In other words, there are seven years remaining in the second age of time dealing with the nation of Israel, which is why this nation is being supernaturally preserved by God during this present third age, simply because God is not yet finished outworking His plan of the ages through the believers of that nation. These seven years remaining is a time of God's judgment against all unbelievers of earth and is approximately covered by Revelation 6:1 to Revelation 19:21 in God's word, although also mentioned often in prophecy in the Bible.

What also needs to be mentioned and is important to remember is that the reason God has a series of ages in time is in order to show us just how sinful the human race is and just how incapable it is of doing good, in terms of pleasing God on its own apart from God. What is meant here is that God's revelation of Himself increases as time progresses, so that those living in the fourth age of time, as compared to the first age of time, will have a far greater knowledge of God.

In other words, as each age progresses, God makes it easier and easier for human beings on earth to come to know Him and to serve Him out of love for Him. For example, in the first two ages, God's precious Son had not yet come to earth, so that He was foreshadowed only through types, such as the animal sacrifices and offerings, and in prophecy. Human beings at that time also only had the Old Testament as light to guide them.

But by the time we reach the fourth age of time, God's precious Son will not only have come from Heaven to earth bodily, but will actually be in the city just above the earth that God will have brought down from Heaven to start the fourth age (noting Revelation 20:10), reigning over the nations as King from there!

Please note what God says at Isaiah 11:9 in part, as just one example of what it will be like in the fourth age, which is something that could not be said in any prior age, "…For the earth will be full of the knowledge of the Lord as the waters cover the sea." What this means then is that when God's final judgment of time comes, relating to all the unbelievers of time (noting Revelations 20:11-15), then none of these unbelievers of time will be able to stand before God and give any excuse for their sin of unbelief, in having personally and freely rejected God's offer of salvation found in His own precious Son, The Lord Jesus Christ. And so, each succeeding age adds to mankind's culpability before a Holy and altogether Righteous God, so that in the end "every mouth may be closed and all the world may become accountable to God" (noting Romans 3:19 in part).

ADDENDUM B

/ The two comings from Heaven to earth of God's precious Son, our Lord Jesus Christ

Another very important truth to know here is that God's word, the Bible, mentions two comings of God's precious Son, The Lord Jesus Christ, from Heaven to earth. His first coming from Heaven to earth was for the purpose of taking on a body like ours, only in the innocence of Adam and as born of a virgin, so as not to incur our sinful nature; and then after living thirty-three and half years on earth carrying out only the will of God His Father in absolute sinlessness out of love for Him, was given over into the hands of unbelievers to be put to death on a cross, before being buried, then resurrected from the dead the third day. And of course, His death was not due to anything God's precious Son, The Lord Jesus Christ, had ever done wrong, but rather was to pay the penalty due the sins of the whole human race, which was death, in order that God might have a basis by which to forgive the sins and grant eternal life to those who come to believe in Him.

Then the second coming of God's precious Son is to be seen as being in two stages. The first stage of His second coming is at the end of this present third age of time, and is for the purpose of bringing to Heaven all believers of earth before God's judgment falls on the unbelievers of the earth, thereby bringing the present third age to a close. God has this first stage in view especially at 1 Thessalonians 4:14-17, although also mentioned in many portions of the New Testament.

Then the second stage of the second coming of God's precious Son, The Lord Jesus Christ, occurs at the end of the seven years of God's judgment, which will end the second age of time. God's precious Son would now be coming for one key battle against God's foes, as led by the devil, before establishing His reign on earth as King during the fourth age of time. This is again disclosed by God in many portions of God's word in the New Testament, but especially in passages such as Matthew 24 and Revelation 19:11-21.

"Jesus said to him, "I am the way, and the truth, and the life; no one comes to the Father but through Me." "

John 14:6

ADDENDUM C

/ For those who may not as yet know God

Possibly you have been reading this book and have become aware of not knowing this God Who created us and gave us physical life into this world, and up to now has allowed you to live on earth. However, now you do have the desire to know God in a personal way. If this is the case, then this Addendum has been written specifically for you!

And what God wants you to have in coming to know Him is the peace and joy, which comes in knowing that all of your sins committed in your lifetime are forgiven and that you have eternal life with God. And so, your greatest need at the moment is to make peace with God so as to go to Heaven, which is God's home. And so, this Addendum will help to bring that about by pointing you to God so as to come to know Him through faith in His Son, The Lord Jesus Christ.

As we begin, we need to note a most important promise which God makes at Romans 6:23 to all those who do not yet know Him, "For the wages of sin is death, but the free gift of God is eternal life in Christ Jesus our Lord." The good news here is that God offers you eternal life with Him as a free gift, which is to be obtained in His Son, Jesus Christ. What God does not do in this verse from the Bible is tell us 'how' to obtain that eternal life with Him.

Another verse which we can look at where God does let us know 'how' one can obtain that eternal life with Him is noting what God tells us at John 3:16, "For God so loved the world, that He gave His only begotten Son, that whoever believes in Him shall not perish, but have eternal life." Now the added truth which God makes known here is that the eternal life, which He gives to a human being as a free gift, is for those who believe in His Son.

Then the question is: What is it that I am to believe about God's Son, Jesus Christ, which will lead God to give me eternal life with Him forever? And the beauty of God is that He never leaves us guessing, especially when it comes to having a personal relationship with Him, which He desires us to have. Therefore, we should not be surprised when God gives us the answer to our question in what He tells us at 1 Corinthians 15:1-4, "[1] Now I make known to you, brethren, the gospel (which is God's good news regarding His Son) which I preached to you, which also you received, in which also you stand, [2] by which also you are saved, if you hold fast the word which I preached to you, unless you believed in vain. [3] For I delivered to you as of first importance what I also received, that Christ died for our sins according to the Scriptures, [4] and that He was buried, and that He was raised on the third day according to the Scriptures…"

Therefore, "the gospel," which simply means 'good news,' which God wants you to hear and believe in order to "be saved," which simply refers to you coming to know God and have eternal life with Him, is that His Son has already died for you, has already been buried, and has already been raised from the dead again the third day after His death, in order that God would have a basis by which to forgive you of all your sins, which are all against Him, and to freely give you eternal life with Him, for simply believing this message in your heart.

One thing which often prevents a person from believing the gospel at this point is not seeing oneself as a sinner before a Holy God. When we look at ourselves by our own assessment, and especially when we compare ourselves with others around us, we often think of ourselves as being better than others, and so good enough to enter Heaven in our present condition. The problem with this is that it is the product of our own thinking and is not God's assessment of our situation!

God's assessment of our situation is as He tells us at Romans 3:10-12,23 in part, "[10] as it is written, "There is none righteous, not even one… [11] there is none who seeks for God [12] all have turned aside… there is none who does good, there is not even one... [23] for all have sinned and fall short of the glory of God…" Quite a different assessment of the human race from that which we as human beings often have of ourselves, is this not? But why would God have such an assessment of the whole human race? For the answer to that question, we need to be aware that God is Creator of all that exists, so that when God created the first man, Adam, at the beginning of time, God created him in innocence, meaning that Adam as first created by God neither knew good nor evil, nor was there any sin anywhere in God's original sinless creation.

However, the day came when God tested Adam with a command, saying to him in the garden of Eden here on earth, which was the perfect environment which God had for him, what we now read at Genesis 2:16,17, "[16] The Lord God commanded the man, saying, "From any tree of the garden you may eat freely; [17] but from the tree of the knowledge of good and evil you shall not eat, for in the day that you eat from it you will surely die." How important to see here that God gave Adam, who although a real person was also representative of the whole human race, the warning of the penalty of death for disobedience to His command.

Unfortunately, the day did come when Adam did partake of the forbidden tree and thereby did sin against God. The moment that happened, Adam not only became a sinner by practice, but also a sinner by nature. One thing my parents had to continually do while under their care was to restrain me from continually going the wrong way, for it seemed that of myself I could not do good, but kept going into sin. The reason this was happening is that from the age of accountability onwards, I had not only become a sinner by practice, but also a sinner by nature.

And here the age of accountability needs to be seen as being when as a young child in innocence – which moment is known only by God – one comes to learn the right from the wrong and chooses the wrong, thereby becoming personally accountable to God for one's own sin against Him, since all sin is first of all against Him. And that is why God can say at Romans 3:23 above that "all have sinned and fall short of the glory of God," because God knows that all human beings will go the way of Adam, our representative man, which is also why God can say what He does in regards to the whole of the human race at Romans 5:12, where we read, "Therefore, just as through one man (Adam) sin entered into the world, and death through sin, and so death spread to all men, because all sinned" (from the age of accountability onward). And so, we see that the whole human race is declared by God to not only be sinners by practice and by nature from the age of accountability onwards, but the whole of the human race is now subject to death! In other words, in God's sight the whole of the human race is under the judgment of the penalty of death, due to all being sinners by practice and by nature.

You will recall above, in the first verse we quoted from Romans 6:23, God did say there that "the wages of sin is death." And what God means by "death" here is not just loss of physical life, as when the physical body we have dies; but also has spiritual death in mind, which is far worse! Spiritual death has its beginning when a separation takes place between a person and God at the moment one becomes a sinner at the age of accountability and ends after the final judgment of time, when God forever casts away from His Presence those who before physical death refused to believe in His Son, The Lord Jesus Christ, thereby personally forfeiting the forgiveness of their sins and eternal life with God. And now all such will pay the penalty for their own sins in hell, away from the Presence of God forever.

It is in the midst of such a hopeless situation in which the whole of the human race found itself in that God TOOK THE INITIATIVE and sent His own eternally existing Son into the world, as born of a virgin in the innocence of Adam – so as not to inherit the sinful nature passed on from generation after generation from Adam onwards through the conception of the female – so that He might be the acceptable sacrifice offered to God His Father at the cross, there bearing our sins in His body, and there dying the death due our sins! God's Son, Jesus Christ, was then buried and raised from the dead the third day, to ever be alive, for it is through Him, on the basis of what God has done for us through His Son, that God The Father forgives our sins and imparts us eternal life.

Now, by God's grace and His enablement, may you see your need of God's Son to be Your Savior from the penalty due sin, which is death, not only physical, but also spiritual. And by God's grace, may He lead you to believe in His Son, Jesus Christ, and in believing, to receive the forgiveness of your sins and eternal life with God forever! And based on the truth just shared, the author would now like to ask you a few questions, with the answer being just between yourself and God:

When God says at Romans 3:23, "for all have sinned and fall short of the glory of God," does that include you?

When God says at Romans 5:8, "But God demonstrates His own love toward us, in that while we were yet sinners, Christ died for us," were you included in Christ's death on behalf of sinners?

And when God further says at 1 Peter 3:18 in part, "For Christ also died for sins once for all, the just for the unjust, so that He might bring us to God, having been put to death in the flesh, but made alive in the spirit," were you part of the unjust for whom Christ died?

When God says at Romans 6:23, "For the wages of sin is death, but the free gift of God is eternal life in Christ Jesus our Lord," do you want that eternal life as a free gift from God?

When God says at John 3:16, "For God so loved the world, that He gave His only begotten Son, that whoever believes in Him shall not perish, but have eternal life," do you now believe that Jesus Christ is indeed God's Son in human flesh, Who came from Heaven to this earth to die in your place, so as to save you from ever experiencing the judgment of God leading to an eternal separation from God in hell?

And when God then further says to you at Isaiah 55:6, "Seek the Lord while He may be found; call upon Him while He is near," for His further promise to you here is as we read at Romans 10:9-11,13, "[9] that if you confess with your mouth Jesus as Lord, and believe in your heart that God raised Him from the dead, you will be saved (that is, you will now enter into a personal relationship with God by faith); [10] for with the heart a person believes, resulting in righteousness (that is, in now receiving God's own righteous and eternal life to live by), and with the mouth he confesses, resulting in salvation (that is, in now receiving as a free gift the forgiveness of sins and eternal life with God). [11] For the Scripture says, "Whoever believes in Him will not be disappointed…" [13] for "Whoever will call on the name of the Lord will be saved." Will you now call upon God from your heart to save you?

The author's prayer for you at this point, as you now call upon God by His grace, is what we read at Romans 15:13, "Now may the God of hope fill you with all joy and peace in believing, so that you will abound in hope by the power of the Holy Spirit."

/ The next book

As this book is being published, God has given His servant the go-ahead to write another book, titled "God's First Letter To The Corinthians." In case it is not the next book, the reader may want to check with the author's website to see what book has been published:

http://www.pilgrimpathwaypublications.com

If you have found this book profitable, or any other of the author's books, please feel free to let family, friends, and co-workers know about this book and the other books. The author is not on any social media sites, so he relies on God and readers to spread the word. May God bless you for doing so!